SpringerBriefs in Law

SpringerBriefs present concise summaries of cutting-edge research and practical applications across a wide spectrum of fields. Featuring compact volumes of 50 to 125 pages, the series covers a range of content from professional to academic. Typical topics might include:

- A timely report of state-of-the art analytical techniques
- A bridge between new research results, as published in journal articles, and a contextual literature review
- A snapshot of a hot or emerging topic
- A presentation of core concepts that students must understand in order to make independent contributions

SpringerBriefs in Law showcase emerging theory, empirical research, and practical application in Law from a global author community. SpringerBriefs are characterized by fast, global electronic dissemination, standard publishing contracts, standardized manuscript preparation and formatting guidelines, and expedited production schedules.

Pablo Castillo-Ortiz

Judicial Governance and Democracy in Europe

 Springer

Pablo Castillo-Ortiz
School of Law
University of Sheffield
Sheffield, UK

ISSN 2192-855X ISSN 2192-8568 (electronic)
SpringerBriefs in Law
ISBN 978-3-031-20189-9 ISBN 978-3-031-20190-5 (eBook)
https://doi.org/10.1007/978-3-031-20190-5

© The Author(s) 2023. This book is an open access publication.
Open Access This book is licensed under the terms of the Creative Commons Attribution 4.0 International License (http://creativecommons.org/licenses/by/4.0/), which permits use, sharing, adaptation, distribution and reproduction in any medium or format, as long as you give appropriate credit to the original author(s) and the source, provide a link to the Creative Commons license and indicate if changes were made.

The images or other third party material in this book are included in the book's Creative Commons license, unless indicated otherwise in a credit line to the material. If material is not included in the book's Creative Commons license and your intended use is not permitted by statutory regulation or exceeds the permitted use, you will need to obtain permission directly from the copyright holder.

The use of general descriptive names, registered names, trademarks, service marks, etc. in this publication does not imply, even in the absence of a specific statement, that such names are exempt from the relevant protective laws and regulations and therefore free for general use.

The publisher, the authors, and the editors are safe to assume that the advice and information in this book are believed to be true and accurate at the date of publication. Neither the publisher nor the authors or the editors give a warranty, expressed or implied, with respect to the material contained herein or for any errors or omissions that may have been made. The publisher remains neutral with regard to jurisdictional claims in published maps and institutional affiliations.

This Springer imprint is published by the registered company Springer Nature Switzerland AG
The registered company address is: Gewerbestrasse 11, 6330 Cham, Switzerland

A la abuela Magdalena

Acknowledgements

The background work for the preparation of this book was carried out in the context of the project 'JURI-POLICY', funded by Research England, Quality-Related (QR) Strategic Priorities Fund. The book was published Open Access thanks to the funding of the University of Sheffield Institutional Open Access Fund. I thank both funders for their support.

An earlier draft of this research was presented at the virtual conference 'Changing the Architecture of Separation of Powers Without an Architect', organized in 2021 by the Judicial Studies Institute of Masaryk University. It was also presented at the American Political Science Association 2021 Annual Meeting. I would like to express my gratitude to the organizers and participants in the events, as well as to Justine Bendel, Paul Cardwell, Juan Mayoral, Rosa Navarrete and Rubén Pérez Trujillano for their comments on earlier versions of this manuscript. I am also indebted to the series editors and peer reviewers of this book for very constructive comments. And I want to thank the staff of the Icelandic Dómstólasýslan for the information provided about the functions and composition of this institution.

Finally, I would like to thank iCourts, at the University of Copenhagen, for hosting me as a Visiting Fellow during the last phase of the work that led to this book.

All mistakes and omissions are the sole responsibility of the author.

Contents

1 **Introduction. Democracy and Judicial Governance in Europe** 1
   1.1   Judicial Governance in Europe 1
   1.2   What is 'Judicial Governance'? 2
   1.3   The Judicial Council Model 2
   1.4   The Courts Service Model 3
   1.5   The Ministry of Justice Model 4
   1.6   Other Models and Other Aspects of Judicial Governance 5
   1.7   Judicial Governance and Democratic Quality in Europe 5
   1.8   The Debate on the Merits of Models of Judicial Governance
        and on their Relationship with Democracy 8
   1.9   Judicial Governance and Democracy: Some Preliminary
        Analyses 9
   1.10 Object and Aims of This Book 11
   1.11 Structure of the Book 13
   References 14

2 **The Trade-Offs of Judicial Governance** 17
   2.1   Introduction 17
   2.2   Independent or Accountable Organs for Judicial Governance 18
   2.3   Powerful or Harmless Organs for Judicial Governance 20
   2.4   A Typology of Institutions 20
   2.5   Ideal Types and Practical Examples 23
        2.5.1 Powerful and Formally Independent: The Hegemonic
              European Model 23
        2.5.2 Independent and Managerial: The Standard Courts
              Service Model 25

		2.5.3	Powerful but Politically Appointed: Politicized Judicial Councils	26
		2.5.4	The Residual Type: Managerial and Politically Appointed	27
	2.6	Powers, Independence, and Democratic Quality		27
	2.7	Conclusion: Towards the Best Imperfect Model for Judicial Governance		29
	References			30
3	**Modernization, Democracy, and Judicial Governance**			33
	3.1	Introduction		33
	3.2	The Political Origins of Organs for Judicial Governance		34
	3.3	Modernization, Democracy, and Judicial Governance		37
	3.4	Methods		39
	3.5	Judicial Governance and Democratic Quality: A Statistical Approach		42
	3.6	Conclusion		43
	References			44
4	**Independent Judicial Councils and Democratic Quality: A Set-Theoretical Approach**			47
	4.1	Introduction		47
	4.2	Modernization, New Institutionalism, and the Role of Judiciaries in Democratic Quality. Theory and Configurational Hypotheses		48
	4.3	Methods		51
	4.4	Analysis of Necessary Conditions		54
	4.5	Analyses of Sufficient Conditions		56
	4.6	Conclusion		58
	References			59
5	**Conclusions and Some Policy Reflections**			61
	5.1	The Complex Relationship Between Judicial Governance and Democracy: Summary of Findings of This Research		61
	5.2	Some Evidence-Based Policy Reflections		62
		5.2.1	Ensuring Independent, Non-corrupt Judiciaries	62
		5.2.2	The Judicial Council Model is not a Bad Arrangement after all …	63
		5.2.3	… but Alternatives to the Judicial Council Model Should not be Discarded	64
	5.3	'Then, are We Sure that We Understand the Relation Between Judicial Governance and Democracy'. Limitations of this Research and Future Research Challenges		65
		5.3.1	Judicial Governance Beyond Democratic Quality	66
	5.4	Judicial Governance Matters		67
	References			68

Appendix A: Classification and Justification of Models of Judicial Governance 69

Appendix B: Database for Replication of Statistical Analyses 81

Appendix C: QCA Data Matrix for Replication of Analyses 87

References 91

Chapter 1
Introduction. Democracy and Judicial Governance in Europe

1.1 Judicial Governance in Europe

Judicial governance is becoming one of the central topics of political discussion in many European countries. In Spain, the renewal of members of the *Consejo General del Poder Judicial*—the Spanish judicial council—has in the last years become one of the main elements of tension between government and opposition. Until recently, Finland was an outlier in the Nordic context, but the creation of the National Court Administration has recently ended this situation. In Poland, judicial governance is at the core of a process of rule of law deterioration which has been thoroughly analysed in the academic literature.[1]

All these cases, though radically different from one another, have something in common. They show the importance that mechanisms for judicial governance are acquiring in contemporary European democracies. They illustrate that these mechanisms are integrated into power dynamics between government and opposition, between branches of government, and even between the national and supranational levels of governance. Contemporary European democracies, both when they are healthy and when they decay, cannot be understood anymore without analysing the role played by institutions such as judicial councils and courts services. This book is precisely about judicial governance and its relationship with democracy as a system of government.

More specifically, this book investigates the relationship between judicial governance and democratic quality. It seeks to make a contribution to our understanding of how different designs of judicial governance relate to the quality of democracy in European countries. Relying on a dataset of 46 European countries, the book uses different methodological tools to investigate this relationship. The analysis underlines the complexity of the relationship between judicial governance and democratic quality in Europe. Such relationships are nuanced, and often differ from country to country.

---

[1] Drinóczi and Bień-Kacała (2019); Pech and Scheppele (2017); Sadurski (2019).

1.2 What is 'Judicial Governance'?

Judicial governance is essential to the role of judiciaries in democracies. It consists of a number of functions and roles that have a strong impact on court systems. Judicial governance is about how to recruit judges, and by whom. It is about how and when to impose disciplinary sanctions on them. It is about how to administer, manage, and finance the judicial branch, and about how to ensure its independence and efficiency.

Models of judicial governance are, however, diverse. In Europe, different countries have opted for different approaches to the governance of their court systems, creating diverse institutions and entrusting competences on judicial governance to different actors. This diversity is valuable from a methodological perspective, and in this research it will allow comparisons between different systems.

Traditionally, decisions on important issues such as the appointment of judges were handled by politicians, and sometimes by judges themselves.[2] The emergence of organs of judicial governance has changed this picture. In their piece on the subject, Bobek and Kosar provided a classification of models of judicial governance in contemporary Europe that has proved particularly useful.[3] Adapting such a taxonomy, European countries can be classified into at least three ideal types: the Ministry of Justice model, the courts service model, and the judicial council model. In the Ministry of Justice model, competences over judicial governance are retained by the executive branch. Contrary to this, the judicial council and the courts service models entrust functions of judicial governance to independent organs. The main difference between them is that judicial councils have powers over the careers of judges—for instance, appointments, disciplinary sanctions, or promotions—while courts services only have general managerial competences over the judicial branch.[4]

1.3 The Judicial Council Model

Judicial councils are characterized as separate institutions with powers over judicial careers. Furthermore, generally, judicial councils are constitutionalized, meaning that the national constitution regulates aspects of these institutions such as their powers and composition. This being said, the fact is that constitutions do not always provide all the details about the composition and functioning of judicial councils. In Spain, for instance, the 1978 Constitution only mentions a few of the competences of the organ and provides only a basic regulation of the mechanism of appointment of members, many of the aspects of the *Consejo General del Poder Judicial* being regulated by the *Ley Orgánica del Poder Judicial*. Similar is the case of France, where several aspects of the *Conseil Supérieur de la Magistrature* are regulated by legislation.[5] Garoupa and Ginsburg argue that the issue of constitutionalization of

---

[2] Garoupa and Ginsburg (2015), p. 106.
[3] Bobek and Kosar (2014).
[4] Ibid., p. 1265 ff.
[5] Garoupa and Ginsburg (2015), p. 119.

judicial governance matters because 'if the composition and powers of the council are left to ordinary law (...) they are subject to enhanced manipulation by the government and legislature and hence have a weaker guarantee of independence', to the point that the authors found evidence of 'systematically lower independence scores for countries with nonconstitutionalized councils'.[6]

As already explained, judicial councils are characterized as concentrating powers over judicial governance, and in particular for having powers over judicial careers in aspects such as appointments, promotions, or disciplinary sanctions on judges. This is not to say that judicial councils control judicial careers in an arbitrary manner. In many countries, the opposite is true, with the system of access to judicial careers or the circumstances in which sanctions can be imposed are strictly regulated.

Additionally, judicial councils often have powers over the management of the judiciary. This is the main area of overlap between judicial councils and courts services (see next section). While the main competences of courts service institutions are managerial, in the case of judicial councils, managerial powers are only part of their many attributions. These managerial competences reach aspects such as the control of the computer software used by the judiciary, receiving citizens' complaints related to the justice system, and management of judicial workloads.

Finally, it is worth noting that judicial councils are often entrusted with other powers in national legal systems. For instance, the Spanish judicial council has the capacity to appoint two of the twelve constitutional judges of the Spanish Constitutional Court.

1.4 The Courts Service Model

Courts services are 'intermediary organizations' whose main function is 'in the area of administration (supervision of judicial registry offices, caseloads and case stocks, flow rates, the promotion of legal uniformity, quality case, etc.), court management (housing, automation, recruitment, training, etc.), and budgeting of the courts'.[7]

Like judicial councils, courts services are formally separate from the political branches of government. Unlike judicial councils, however, courts services do not generally have a wide range of powers over judicial careers, and their competences are mostly managerial. These competences are focused on what Garoupa and Ginsburg call 'housekeeping functions' which are 'designed to prevent moral hazard: by insulating the judiciary from the management of resources, the council prevents corruption or distraction from the core task of judging'.[8]

---

[6] Ibid., p. 129.
[7] Bobek and Kosar (2014), p. 1266.
[8] Garoupa and Ginsburg (2015), p. 110.

Since courts services do not concentrate all competences over judicial governance together, the question that arises immediately is that of *who* holds the remaining powers. As those remaining powers refer to aspects as important as the appointment or sanctioning of judges, the question is a highly pertinent one to understand the interaction of this system of judicial governance with democracy. In some cases, like Denmark, Ireland, or Scotland, the courts service model is combined with special bodies for judicial appointments.[9] Such bodies can be themselves independent and protect judicial independence.

1.5 The Ministry of Justice Model

The Ministry of Justice model has been defined as 'the longest-standing model. Under this framework, the Ministry of Justice plays a key role in both the appointment and promotion of judges and in the administration of courts and court management'.[10] For instance, in the Czech Republic, the Ministry of Justice has the *de jure* powers to appoint and dismiss court presidents.[11]

The existence of a Ministry of Justice model, however, does not always mean that the executive monopolizes all powers over judicial governance. As put by Kosař 'even in countries where political branches still have the major say (Austria, Czechia, and Germany), the power of judges in judicial governance has increased gradually'.[12] According to the author, 'Czech as well as German judges, each group in its own way, have been very influential in governing the judiciary, despite the nominally prevailing Ministry of Justice model'.[13]

These constraints on ministerial power over the judiciary in the Ministry of Justice model are often political, rather than strictly legal. In the Czech Republic, for instance, the Ministry of Justice rarely uses its power to dismiss court presidents, given the political costs of this action as well as the ministerial reliance on court presidents to conduct policy and make well-informed decisions about judicial careers.[14]

---

[9] Kosař (2018), p. 1574.
[10] Bobek and Kosar (2014), p. 1265.
[11] David Kosař (2017), p. 105.
[12] Kosař (2018), p. 1574.
[13] Ibid., p. 1587.
[14] David Kosař (2017), p. 106.

1.6 Other Models and Other Aspects of Judicial Governance

Of course, there are other approaches to judicial governance beyond the judicial council, courts service, and Ministry of Justice models. This is partly because many countries in Europe have *sui generis* or hybrid approaches to judicial governance. But also because in regions beyond Europe, we can find other approaches to the governance of the judiciary. For instance, Israel relies on a model centred around a Director of Courts, which Lurie, Reichman, and Sagy define as 'an administrative entity that "manages" the judiciary' and which, in important respects, 'may be regarded as a regulator of judges'.[15] In many Latin American countries, a Supreme Court model has historically existed, based on the powers of these institutions over judicial careers.[16]

Furthermore, an increasing body of literature is starting to show that even in Europe there is more to judicial governance than judicial councils, courts services, and Ministries of Justice.[17] These other aspects include the role of court presidents and chief justices, in a field that is more decentralized than the classification into ideal models used in this book suggests. In acknowledging the limitations of the approach taken, however, this book remains focused on these broad ideal types. The reason is that these general models still seem to define the approaches to judicial governance in the countries under examination. The cross-country diversity in approaches to judicial governance in the sample of this book can be very well captured by these ideal types, and this cross-country variation can in turn become a fruitful source of comparisons.

1.7 Judicial Governance and Democratic Quality in Europe

This book provides a comprehensive study of models for judicial governance in European countries. In providing for such comprehensive analysis, the research contributes to the task of correcting what Kosař has identified as one of the drawbacks of literature in English in the field: its focus on judicial councils in Central and Eastern Europe 'which frames the debate and gives it (owing to the specifics of post-communist judiciaries) a peculiar shape'.[18] The research is cross-sectional, focused on a specific moment in time: late 2021 and early 2022, in order to capture the latest dynamics of judicial governance in Europe at the time in which this book was prepared.

---

[15] Lurie et al. (2020).
[16] See, for instance, Pozas-Loyo and Rios-Figueroa (2010).
[17] See, for instance, Kosař and Spáč (2021) and Šipulová et al. (2022).
[18] Kosař (2018), p. 1586.

Table 1.1 Models of judicial governance in Europe

	Judicial council	Courts service	Ministry of justice	Hybrid/other
High liberal democracy score	*Estonia*, France, *Greece*, Italy, Lithuania, Portugal, Slovakia, Spain	Belgium, Denmark, Finland, Iceland, Ireland, Latvia, Netherlands, Norway, Sweden, UK*	Austria, Czechia, Germany	Cyprus, Luxembourg, Switzerland
Intermediate liberal democracy score	Albania, Bosnia and Herzegovina, Croatia, Georgia, Bulgaria, Moldova, North Macedonia, Montenegro, *Poland*, Romania, Slovenia, Ukraine, Kosovo	Malta		Armenia, Hungary
Low liberal democracy score	Serbia, Turkey		Belarus	Azerbaijan, Kazakhstan, Russia
N	23	11	4	8
Share	50%	24%	9%	17%

*Includes the organs for judicial governance of England and Wales, Scotland, and Northern Ireland. In italics, weak form of judicial councils

Own elaboration

Table 1.1 constitutes to the best of this author's knowledge the first attempt at exhaustively classifying European countries into these different models of judicial governance.[19] It is important to note that any classification of real-world cases into ideal types is difficult and potentially invites contestation. The reason is that these real-world cases often exhibit features of hybridity and idiosyncrasy that make the taxonomy very difficult. However, in order to justify my classification, the reader can find at the end of this book Appendix A with information—and sources—about each country.

As shown in Table 1.1 the most frequent model of judicial governance in the European continent is currently the judicial council model, which has been implemented in 50% of the countries analysed. The courts service model is however far from residual. It exists in 24% of the countries covered by my sample. The Ministry of Justice model does seem to be exceptional, existing only in four instances that together represent 9% of the countries of the sample. Finally, eight countries have been classified as *sui generis* or fully hybrid models.

---

[19] The table includes European countries. The smallest countries (i.e., those with a population smaller than 100.000 inhabitants) are excluded, given their sui generis political and judicial dynamics (Andorra, Monaco, Liechtenstein, San Marino, and Vatican City). Armenia, Azerbaijan, Georgia, Kazakhstan, Russia and Turkey are included.

1.7 Judicial Governance and Democratic Quality in Europe

Some countries in Table 1.1 were particularly difficult to classify. In line with previous research on organs for judicial governance,[20] the subtype of 'weak Judicial Councils' was created to acknowledge the existence of institutions that have certain powers over judicial careers but overall have very reduced competences. These are cases of judicial councils that are close to the courts service model.

Table 1.1 also classifies countries into groups by level of democracy quality, following the V-Dem Liberal Democracy Index v. 11.[21] This provides some preliminary information about the relationship between models of judicial governance and democracy.[22] For the group of countries with a high liberal democracy index, a wide variation can be observed, with all models of judicial governance being represented. But it also can be observed that in the case of countries with an intermediate liberal democracy score, the judicial council model is clearly overrepresented. And in the case of countries with a low liberal democracy score, what is most striking is that the courts service model is absent from the group.

Organs for judicial governance are central to the functioning of political systems. But the actual role of organs for judicial governance in a polity does not only depend on the type of institution implemented (in columns in Table 1.1) but also on the level of democratic quality of the system as a whole (in rows in Table 1.1). As we move downwards in the table, countries start exhibiting a lower quality of democracy. An interesting question is whether this translates into organs for judicial governance more subservient to political actors. For instance, countries such as Poland and Hungary were particularly difficult to classify. In these countries, the institutions under examination exist in a well-documented context of rule of law backsliding.[23] This translates into a very *sui generis* functioning of the organs for judicial governance.

A first, important conclusion can be thus formulated at this point: similar organs for judicial governance can play different roles in a political system depending on the institutional set-up in which they are inserted. Both Poland and Italy have been classified as having a judicial council—even if it is of the weak type in Poland—but the functioning of the judicial branch could not be more dissimilar in these two countries. Both in Austria and Belarus, the executive keeps important powers over judicial careers, but the role that the judiciary plays in these political systems is hugely different, Austria being a healthy democracy while Belarus is, at the time of writing, a dictatorship without regard for the rule of law. This is why, for each case, attention to detail matters. Judicial governance exists in a wider legal and political setting which can modify the way the judiciary works in the system. And even for apparently similar organs for judicial governance, certain aspects of institutional design and the institutional context might make an important difference.

---

[20] Castillo-Ortiz (2019).

[21] Coppedge et al. (2021) V-Dem Codebook v.11.1.

[22] Countries scoring between 0 and 0.33 are included in the group of low liberal democracy score. Intermediate liberal democracy score represents countries scoring between 0.34 and 0.66. Countries with scores between 0.67 and 1 are included in the group of countries with a high liberal democracy score.

[23] Drinóczi and Bień-Kacała (2019); Halmai (2018); Pech and Scheppele (2017); Sadurski (2019); Bugarič and Ginsburg (2016).

1.8 The Debate on the Merits of Models of Judicial Governance and on their Relationship with Democracy

As the diffusion of the different contemporary models for judicial governance is relatively recent, the debate on the respective merits of each model has only gained momentum in recent years. Furthermore, a large part of the debate is, as acknowledged by Garoupa and Ginsburg,[24] often based on theoretical assumptions rather than on comprehensive evidence.

In Europe, a key theme of this debate has been focused more particularly on the benefits and drawbacks of the judicial council model. For a long time, the standard position seemed to be the agreement on the benefits of this approach to judicial governance. According to Kosař, 'a significant part of the policy guidelines and scholarship on judicial self-governance suffers from *normative bias*, as many scholars and policymakers have presumed that the rise of judicial self-governance is a one-way path and an unquestionable good'.[25]

Against this background, a body of literature has recently emerged showing scepticism about the performance of organs for judicial governance. In their work, Voigt and El-Bialy found that countries with separate institutions for judicial governance have less efficient judiciaries, which were capable of resolving less cases.[26] Popova has recently provided evidence that judicial empowerment through mechanisms of self-government might not lead to behavioural change on the part of judges.[27] Focusing on the case of Slovakia, Kosař and Spáč show that the creation of a judicial council in this country did not prevent political control over Chief Justices, with important implications for the rule of law.[28] Furthermore, literature has suggested that judicial councils can reduce democratic accountability and increase corporatism of judges, thus leading to counterproductive outcomes.[29] Garoupa and Ginsburg tested the impact of organs for judicial governance on judicial independence, finding a very small effect. According to the authors, 'the conventional wisdom is that they [organs for judicial governance] enhance judicial independence, but we are skeptical of this claim (…). We also found little evidence in favor of the widespread assumption that councils increase quality or independence in the aggregate (…).[30] In Europe, an association of judicial councils has been formed. It seems that judicial councils might reflect the efforts of a kind of transnational movement, seeking to advance a particular model, regardless or not they achieve their desired goals. Judicial independence, in this process, becomes an idea to be wielded in debates rather than a real tangible good'. In a similar vein, in their empirical study, Urbániková and Šipulová

---

[24] Garoupa and Ginsburg (2015), p. 99.
[25] Kosař (2018), p. 1586.
[26] Voigt and El-Bialy (2016).
[27] Popova (2020).
[28] Kosař and Spáč (2021).
[29] Spáč et al. (2018).
[30] Garoupa and Ginsburg (2015), pp. 137–139.

did not find enough evidence that judicial councils manage to improve institutional performance of judicial systems, or public confidence in the judiciary.[31]

Based on a comprehensive review of case studies in Europe, Kosar recently advanced four warnings against the judicial council model.[32] First, precisely because they concentrate powers they are more attractive to politicians, who will be more eager to capture them. Against this, the author argues that a solution could be the diffusion of powers of judicial governance among different bodies. Second, judicial self-governance just transfers the power to new hands, creating new channels of politicization of the judiciary. Third, judicial councils can be captured not only by the outside but also by the inside. Finally, informal networks might also capture judicial self-governance bodies.

The debate on judicial governance is thus, nowadays, far from settled. This book seeks to contribute with evidence-based arguments to the debate. In particular, in this book, I will seek to understand the relationship of different models of judicial governance with the quality of democracy in European countries, using empirical evidence and different analytical techniques.

1.9 Judicial Governance and Democracy: Some Preliminary Analyses

Judicial governance matters because judiciaries play a central role in the functioning of liberal democracies. This role is manifested in at least two aspects of the relationship between courts and politics. First, at the institutional level, courts systems act as a control on the political branches of government, in line with the principles of separation of powers and checks and balances.[33] Judiciaries are expected to offer a means of redress against the actions of politicians, to limit their power and to ensure that they abide by the rule of law. Second, at the substantive level, judiciaries guarantee and enforce the rights of citizens. Rights, which constitute a core element of liberal constitutionalism, would be rendered meaningless if they were unenforceable by independent judicial actors. Systems of judicial governance should ensure that these two functions are correctly carried out by independent judges in the judicial branch.

The relation of systems of judicial governance with democracy is however not straightforward. As I showed previously, different models of judicial governance appear to be associated with different levels of democratic quality. Figure 1.1 and Table 1.2 provide more fine-grained detail about these associations.

---

[31] Urbániková and Šipulová (2018).
[32] Kosař (2018), p. 1591.
[33] Hamilton et al. (2003[1788]), p. 234.

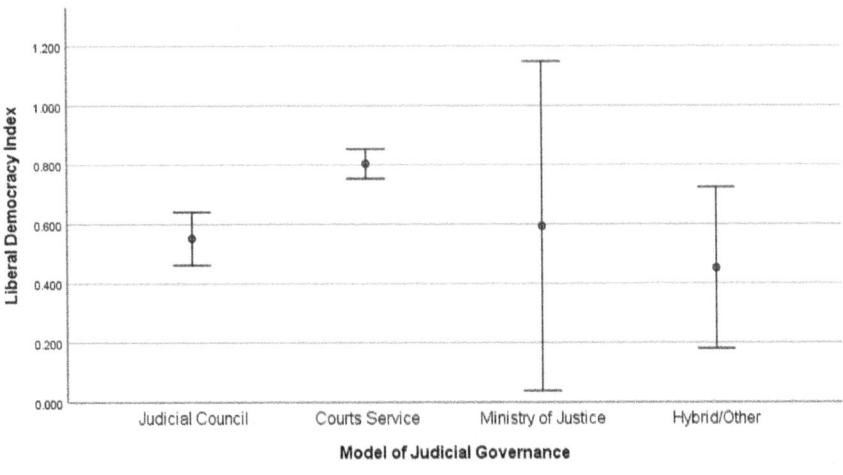

Fig. 1.1 V-Dem liberal democracy index by model of judicial governance

Table 1.2 Correlations (Spearman's rho) between models of judicial governance and democracy indexes[34]

		Liberal democracy index	Electoral democracy index	Equality before the law index
Judicial council	Correlation coefficient	−0.300*	−0.275	−0.364*
	Sig. (2-tailed)	0.043	0.064	0.013
	N	46	46	46
Courts service	Correlation coefficient	0.555**	0.522**	0.539**
	Sig. (2-tailed)	0.000	0.000	0.000
	N	46	46	46
Ministry of justice	Correlation coefficient	0.000	−0.017	0.061
	Sig. (2-tailed)	1.000	0.908	0.687
	N	46	46	46
Hybrid/other	Correlation coefficient	−0.229	−0.212	−0.173
	Sig. (2-tailed)	0.126	0.158	0.251
	N	46	46	46

**Correlation is significant at the 0.01 level (2-tailed)
*Correlation is significant at the 0.05 level (2-tailed)

---

[34] Non-parametric Spearman's rho correlations are used as the data does not follow a normal distribution. Data on models for judicial governance justified in Appendix A.

Own elaboration

Using data from the V-Dem Liberal Democracy Index v.11,[35] Fig. 1.1 shows that countries with a judicial council have on average democracies of worse quality than countries with a courts service.

In Table 1.2, I show the correlations between the four approaches to judicial governance and three different types of indexes of democratic quality from V-Dem v.11[36]: the Liberal Democracy Index, the Electoral Democracy Index, and the Equality Before the Law and Individual Liberty Index.

The correlations between all of these indexes and the different models of judicial governance seem to point in the same direction. In the case of the judicial council model, this approach to judicial governance is negatively associated to all of them, meaning that countries with a judicial council are more likely to have a worse score in the different democratic quality indexes. Something similar happens with the category of hybrid/other models of judicial governance. These negative correlations are significant for the case of the Judicial Council with the Liberal Democracy Index and with the Equality Before the Law Index.

The opposite is true of the courts service model. This model is positively associated with the different indexes of democratic quality. This association is significant and particularly strong in all three indexes. Put differently, in countries with a courts service approach to the management of their judiciary we are more likely to find a better quality of democracy.

Finally, the Ministry of Justice model seems to be scarcely correlated with the different indexes of democratic quality.

1.10 Object and Aims of This Book

Judicial governance and democracy thus interact in complex, paradoxical ways. Institutions like judicial councils have been defended with the argument that they are good for essential aspects of democracy such as judicial independence and the rule of law.[37] However, countries where judicial councils exist fare worse on average in relation to all main indexes of democratic quality. Courts services seemed to be much more positively correlated with democratic quality, despite that they are not the 'standard'[38] option for judicial governance promoted by European institutions. And different approaches to judicial governance, regardless of their original aims, can be found in countries with different levels of democratic quality, sometimes becoming

---

[35] Coppedge et al. (2021) V-Dem Codebook v.11.1.
[36] Ibid.
[37] See Garoupa and Ginsburg (2015), pp. 98–99.
[38] See Bobek and Kosar (2014).

instruments of illiberal governments to consolidate their power.[39] Democracy and judicial governance are thus two phenomena connected in intriguing ways.

This book is about that connection. In exploring it, I will try to provide a response to a general research question: what is the relationship between organs for judicial governance and democratic quality? In responding to such a research question, my findings make a contribution to our understanding of the relationship of organs for judicial governance—especially judicial councils—and democracy. Although countries of the sample based on the judicial council model have on average democracies of worse quality (see Fig. 1.1), I show that this might simply be explained by an omitted variable bias: if we take into account the different levels of economic development of the countries of the sample there does not seem to be a negative effect of having judicial councils on democracy. I explain this through modernization theory. Furthermore, I show that in all instances of low levels of quality of electoral democracy the model of independent judicial councils was absent. My analyses also suggest that, keeping constant other factors such as the level of economic development and EU membership, countries with independent judicial councils—and non-corrupt judiciaries—have better levels of electoral democracy quality than countries without such approach to judicial governance. At the same time, however, my findings also suggest that having an independent judicial council is logically irrelevant to cases of a high quality of electoral democracy: other combinations of factors seem to be more relevant, among them judiciary-related conditions such as high levels of court independence and low levels of judicial corruption.

Focused, therefore, on the relationship between judicial governance and democracy, the book has three different but interconnected aims:

- The first aim of this book is academic. Despite that the book is written—I hope—in an accessible manner, in the following pages I aim to make an academic contribution to our understanding of institutions for judicial governance. To do so, the research will analyse diverse aspects of the relationship between democracy and judicial governance, such as the different trade-offs of design of institutions for judicial governance and their relationship to democracy, or the association between different types of these institutions and indicators of democratic quality. The book thus seeks to advance our knowledge on a very important topic, which is central to the academic, political, and social debates about the organization of the judicial branch: how to build organs for judicial governance that contribute to democratic quality.
- The second aim of this book is policy-oriented. Based on the different analyses carried out in the book, in Chap. 5, I will present some evidence-based policy reflections about organs for judicial governance. These reflections are put forward with the overall objective to improve the capacity of organs for judicial governance to contribute to democratic quality. My findings and reflections refer mostly to Europe, the world region in which I specialize as a researcher and which is the basis of this book. But, taking into account the modest generalizability of the findings

---

[39] See Bugarič and Ginsburg (2016); Pech and Scheppele (2017).

of the research, academics and policymakers in other world regions might find them also useful.
- The third aim of this work is to contribute to public debates. In a moment in which social debate about the appropriate forms to govern judiciaries seems to burgeon, this book aims at presenting the main aspects of this topic to the general public. Some parts of this book are unavoidably more complex and require some methodological background—especially in Chaps. 3 and 4. But in general I have tried to write this book, to the extent that it was possible, in accessible language. Also for this reason, although there are relatively complex empirical analyses throughout the book, these are presented in the clearest and most easily readable way. With this, I hope to contribute to public debates about judicial governance in European countries, providing citizens interested in the topic with tools that hopefully will make such debate more fruitful.

1.11 Structure of the Book

This book is structured as follows. This chapter has introduced the reader into the main topic of the research, the relation between democracy and judicial governance. The chapter has argued that the relationship between judicial governance and democracy is of an extraordinary importance and yet it is also marked by paradoxes. In fact, we know precious little about how democracy and judicial governance interact, especially at the empirical level.

Chapter 2 adds further complexity to the question of the types of design of organs for judicial governance in Europe. In particular, I will build a complementary typology of models of judicial governance that takes into account the degree of independence vis-à-vis political actors of each institution in each country, in addition to their powers. Building on such typology, I will explore the different dilemmas that we confront when designing organs for judicial governance, and how these dilemmas relate to the preservation of democratic systems of government.

Chapters 3 and 4 provide a more fine-grained analysis of the relationship between models of judicial governance and democracy in contemporary Europe. To do so, I will make use of empirical material and of statistical and configurational methods to carry out my analyses.

Throughout the book, thus, I will present information about the relation between democracy and judicial governance, and also about the pros and cons of each system for the government of the judicial branch. In Chap. 5, taking stock of these findings and of the findings of other research in the field, I will present some reflections about models for judicial governance. The main aim of these reflections is to improve the contribution of systems for judicial governance to the better functioning of democratic systems, and also to minimize some trade-offs that are inherent to the design of these institutions.

The final Appendix presents the data used for the empirical analyses that are at the core of my argument.

References

Bobek M, Kosar D (2014) Global solutions, local damages: a critical study in judicial councils in central and Eastern Europe. Ger Law J 15:1257–1292

Bugarič B, Ginsburg T (2016) The assault on postcommunist courts. J Democr 27:69–82

Castillo-Ortiz P (2019) The politics of implementation of the judicial council model in Europe. Eur Polit Sci Rev 11:503–520. https://doi.org/10.1017/S1755773919000298

Coppedge M, Gerring J, Knutsen CH, et al (2021) V-Dem Codebook v.11.1

Drinóczi T, Bień-Kacała A (2019) Illiberal constitutionalism: the case of Hungary and Poland. Ger Law J 20:1140–1166. https://doi.org/10.1017/glj.2019.83

Garoupa N, Ginsburg T (2015) Judicial reputation: a comparative theory. The University of Chicago Press

Halmai G (2018) Illiberal Constitutionalism? The Hungarian Constitution in a European Perspective. In: Kadelbach S (ed) Vergassungskrisen in der Europäischen Union. Nomos, Baden-Baden, pp 85–104

Hamilton A, Madison J, Jay J (2003[1788]) The federalist: with letters of Brutus. Cambridge University Press, Cambridge

Kosař D (2017) Politics of judicial independence and judicial accountability in Czechia: bargaining in the shadow of the law between court presidents and the ministry of justice. Eur Const Law Rev 13:96–123

Kosař D (2018) Beyond judicial councils: forms, rationales and impact of judicial self-governance in Europe. Ger Law J 19:1567–1612. https://doi.org/10.1017/S2071832200023178

Kosař D, Spáč S (2021) Post-communist Chief justices in Slovakia: from transmission belts to semi-autonomous actors? Hague J Rule Law 13:107–142

Lurie G, Reichman A, Sagy Y (2020) Agencification and the administration of courts in Israel. Regul Gov 14:718–740. https://doi.org/10.1111/rego.12236

Pech L, Scheppele KL (2017) Illiberalism within: rule of law backsliding in the EU. Camb Yearb Eur Leg Stud 19:3–47. https://doi.org/10.1017/cel.2017.9

Popova M (2020) Can a leopard change its spots? Strategic behavior versus professional role conception during Ukraine's 2014 court chair elections. Law Policy 42:365–381

Pozas-Loyo A, Rios-Figueroa J (2010) The politics of amendment processes: supreme court influence in the design of judicial councils. Tex Law Rev 89:1807–1834

Sadurski W (2019) Poland's constitutional breakdown. Oxford University Press

Šipulová K, Spáč S, Kosař D, Papoušková T, Derka V (2022) Judicial self-governance index: towards better understanding of the role of judges in governing the judiciary. Regul Gov. https://doi.org/10.1111/rego.12453

Spáč S, Šipulová K, Urbániková M (2018) Capturing the judiciary from inside: the story of judicial self-governance in Slovakia. Ger Law J 19:1741–1768. https://doi.org/10.1017/S2071832200023221

Urbániková M, Šipulová K (2018) Failed expectations: does the establishment of judicial councils enhance confidence in courts? Ger Law J 19:2105–2136. https://doi.org/10.1017/S2071832200023348

Voigt S, El-Bialy N (2016) Identifying the determinants of aggregate judicial performance: taxpayers' money well spent? Eur J Law Econ 41:283–319. https://doi.org/10.1007/s10657-014-9474-8

Open Access This chapter is licensed under the terms of the Creative Commons Attribution 4.0 International License (http://creativecommons.org/licenses/by/4.0/), which permits use, sharing, adaptation, distribution and reproduction in any medium or format, as long as you give appropriate credit to the original author(s) and the source, provide a link to the Creative Commons license and indicate if changes were made.

The images or other third party material in this chapter are included in the chapter's Creative Commons license, unless indicated otherwise in a credit line to the material. If material is not included in the chapter's Creative Commons license and your intended use is not permitted by statutory regulation or exceeds the permitted use, you will need to obtain permission directly from the copyright holder.

Chapter 2
The Trade-Offs of Judicial Governance

2.1 Introduction

In the previous chapter of this book, I began to analyse the relationship between different approaches to judicial governance and democracy. The approaches to judicial governance scrutinized were the judicial council model, the courts service model, and the Ministry of Justice model, in addition to a general category of hybrid and other models. This taxonomy reflects which actors have in each jurisdiction powers over the judicial branch, and what is the extent of those powers.

Such taxonomy, however, ignores an important dimension of judicial governance: the extent to which organs like judicial councils or courts services are independent from political actors. This dimension matters because it can affect the actual role that organs of judicial governance play in a political system. A clear example is that of judicial councils, for which institutional independence becomes crucial. Since judicial councils were created, among other goals, to increase judicial independence,[1] political control over these institutions might undermine their capacity to fulfil this fundamental task. Independence and power are thus two central dimensions for organs of judicial governance, and it is only by taking both into account that we can understand the role and contribution of these institutions to democratic systems.

In fact, these two dimensions are important because they are associated with trade-offs in institutional design. According to Garoupa and Ginsburg, organs for judicial governance face a dilemma between independence and accountability: institutions such as judicial councils were created to increase judicial independence vis-à-vis politicians, but in so doing they partly undermine the accountability of the judicial branch.[2] Additionally, organs for judicial governance face an intersecting trade-off: more powerful institutions are more capable of defending the judiciary from political

---

[1] See Garoupa and Ginsburg (2009a, b).

[2] Ibid.

© The Author(s) 2023
P. Castillo-Ortiz, *Judicial Governance and Democracy in Europe*,
SpringerBriefs in Law, https://doi.org/10.1007/978-3-031-20190-5_2

actors, but in accumulating such powers they might become themselves a threat to the independence of individual judges.[3]

Trade-offs and institutional dilemmas matter because they force us to choose between political values that are important and, simultaneously, mutually exclusive. Such trade-offs compel institutional designers to confront important political choices. In this chapter, I will analyse such dilemmas of design of organs for judicial governance and how they affect the role of these institutions in democratic political systems.

2.2 Independent or Accountable Organs for Judicial Governance

Literature in law and politics suggests that two values are particularly important for judiciaries: independence and accountability. Albeit the independence and accountability of the courts are not the same as those of the organs for judicial governance, the former and the latter may frequently be connected.

Larkins defines independence as conflict resolution by a 'neutral third (...) someone who can be trusted to settle controversies after considering only the facts in relation to relevant laws', a 'judge who has no relation to the litigants and no direct interest in the outcome of the case'.[4] Van Dijk emphasizes that 'it is generally believed that a high degree of judicial independence is necessary for people to appreciate and trust the courts (...). In turn, trust is seen as necessary for courts to be able to function, if only to incite people to bring their disputes to court, to cooperate with the court and to accept judgements willingly'.[5] The independence of the court system seems thus central to its successful operation.

Judicial accountability is more difficult to define, but in general it can be deemed as referring to responsiveness by courts and judges to other actors for their decisions and behaviour. This definition, however, opens two questions: which are the standards that must be used to assess accountable judicial behaviour, and to whom should judges be accountable?

On the first question, Contini and Mohr state that accountability should not be limited to verifying the productivity or efficiency of judges, but should also include values such as legality, equality, independence, and impartiality.[6] On the second question, Burbank argues that judges should be accountable to the public, to politicians, and to the judiciary as an institution.[7] From this perspective, the public matters because it has an interest in proceedings that are open and decisions that are accessible. Accountability to politicians would matter because they fund the court system

---

[3] Castillo-Ortiz (2017).
[4] Larkins (1996), p. 608.
[5] Van Dijk (2021), p. 1.
[6] Contini and Mohr (2008), p. 31.
[7] Burbank (2007), p. 912.

and pass the laws the judges enforce. And accountability to the judiciary as an institution would be relevant because the independence of individual judges exists to protect the independence of the judiciary as a whole.

Both being important judicial-political values, the relationship between independence and accountability is nonetheless controversial. For Burbank, 'judicial independence is merely the other side of the coin from judicial accountability', both being complementary.[8] However, for Garoupa and Ginsburg, the relationship between these two values is more complex: 'while adequate institutions might enhance judicial independence and minimize the problems of a politicized judiciary, increasing the powers and independence enjoyed by judges risks creating the opposite problem of over-judicializing public policy (...) as more and more tasks are given to the judiciary, there is pressure for greater accountability because the judiciary takes over more functions from democratic processes'.[9] The authors describe organs for judicial governance as situated in an intermediate point between total judicial autonomy—with no accountability—and total political control of the judiciary—with no judicial independence.[10] For the authors, accountability requires that 'the judiciary as a whole maintain some level of responsiveness to society, as well as a high level of professionalism and quality on the part of its members'.[11]

The relationship between independence and accountability is thus ambiguous. These two values could be thought of not only as two extremes of a continuum but also as two independent values that might sometimes—yet not always—collide. As suggested by Contini and Mohr, whether there is a trade-off between independence and accountability depends on how we define these concepts.[12] On many levels, independence and accountability can coexist and even reinforce each other. For instance, a judiciary subject to more stringent standards of good practice will gain diffuse support, which it can then use to make decisions that run counter to the preferences of political majorities. But there is at least one dimension in which these two values are in a trade-off relationship in the context of the design of organs for judicial governance: the more independent organs for judicial governance are from political actors, the less accountable they are to them. This causes a tension, because judicial independence is a desirable value, but unaccountable judiciaries can become excessively activist or can incur in bad practices. For instance, it has been argued that accountability would be particularly important in developing countries, as 'leaving the judiciary unchecked by external actors (...) might easily lead to corruption'.[13]

This is therefore the first dilemma of judicial governance. When designing organs for the governance of the judiciary, political actors may opt between having independent organs that are less subject to political accountability, or politically accountable institutions that are less independent than would be desirable.

---

[8] Ibid., pp. 911–912.
[9] Garoupa and Ginsburg (2009a, b), pp. 117–118.
[10] Ibid., p. 106.
[11] Ibid., p. 106.
[12] Contini and Mohr (2008).
[13] Bobek and Kosar (2014), p. 1271.

2.3 Powerful or Harmless Organs for Judicial Governance

The second aspect of institutions for judicial governance that presents important trade-offs is their range of powers. Institutions for judicial governance present a wide variation in the amount of powers that they hold. In principle, institutions with a wide range of powers should be a good thing: in accumulating powers over judicial careers and judicial management, they take these powers away from the hands of political actors, thus maximizing judicial independence. However, there is a downside to having powerful institutions for judicial governance. When these institutions are very powerful they indeed might have the capacity to defend judges from political actors, but this is at the cost of rendering such institutions themselves a potential threat to the independence of individual judges.

A recent study provides some preliminary evidence in this regard. Using an empirical approach, the work showed that countries in which judges felt more frequently that their judicial council had not respected their independence were often countries with strong judicial councils.[14] Therefore, powerful organs for judicial governance also come at a price, as it is these very institutions that might become a threat for the autonomy of individual judges.

This is then the second dilemma of judicial governance. Constitution-makers and policymakers can opt between having strong organs for judicial governance that can become an internal threat for the autonomy of individual judges, or weak institutions that cannot protect judges from external pressures. This is a tragic dilemma, as both options involve sacrificing political-constitutional values that are central to the construction of judiciaries in a healthy democracy.

2.4 A Typology of Institutions

The analysis above identified two trade-offs in the design of organs for judicial governance: the powerful-harmless dilemma and the independent-accountable dilemma. These two theoretical dilemmas translate, in the practice of empirically existing organs for judicial governance, into choices regarding the design of the institutions: organs for judicial governance can be designed as either more or less powerful and as either more independent or more accountable. Furthermore, elements of institutional design intersect: the two dilemmas of the institutional design of organs for judicial governance interact, giving rise to four types or categories of organs.

In order to classify organs for judicial governance into such four categories, I gathered data about such organs in the countries of my sample and assigned values to each country (see Appendix A). For the powerful-disempowered dimension, I took into account whether the organ for judicial governance had significant powers over judicial careers or not. That is to say, I took into account whether it was a judicial council or a courts service institution. Countries following the Ministry of

---

[14] Castillo-Ortiz (2017).

2.4 A Typology of Institutions

Justice model are excluded from the analysis in this part of the research, because in these countries there is no independent organ for judicial governance or this is less relevant. Hybrid approaches are also excluded, as their idiosyncratic features make classification unviable.

For the accountable-independent dimension, I took into account whether a majority of members of the organ had been formally appointed or not by political actors. In this latter regard, my analysis differs from that of Garoupa and Ginsburg, who measure politicization by taking into account how many members of the institution are judges, lawyers, or non-judges, regardless of who appointed them.[15] My operationalization thus focuses essentially on *de jure* independence of the organs for judicial governance vis-à-vis other actors, especially politicians. For this reason, my main source of information on this aspect has been the formal regulation of organs for judicial governance, often contained in constitutional or legal sources. For this point, it is important to recall that *de jure* independence does not always equal *de facto* independence.[16] For instance, this is the case if an institution is in practice controlled by external actors such as politicians, even when its regulation proclaims and even provides formal guarantees of independence. Yet, while both *de jure* and *de facto* independence are important, my focus on the former derives from an interest in studying the impact of formal rules in the practice of these organs and of the polities where they are created.

As with Table 1.1, the operationalization and assignment of values in this chapter made acknowledging that the classification of organs for judicial governance into types is complex, as there are many borderline and ambiguous cases. However, to maximize transparency and rigour, the final Appendix A provides justification and sources for each of the countries classified.

After assigning values to each institution for judicial governance in each of the two dimensions of institutional design, I constructed a Truth Table (Table 2.1). The Truth Table identifies all combinations of the two dimensions of design of organs for judicial governance, indicating which institutions belong to each configuration, as well as the number of cases and share of the total included in each configuration.

Own elaboration (see Appendix A for sources)

As can be seen in Table 2.1, out of those countries with a special organ for judicial governance, the most frequent type is that of powerful and formally independent councils for the judiciary, adding up 53% of the cases. The second most frequent model is that of formally independent courts services (23% of the cases). Powerful but not independent judicial councils comprise 15% of the total, while the proportion of the model of non-independently appointed courts services is 9%.

With the information provided in Table 2.1, some patterns seem to emerge. First, the general picture is one of organs for judicial governance that, at least in their formal design, are politically independent. Judicial councils and courts services that are *de jure* independent add up 76% of the cases. There are however important

---

[15] Garoupa and Ginsburg (2009a, b), p. 122.
[16] See for a discussion Voigt (2021).

Table 2.1 Truth table showing the typology of organs for judicial governance

Powers	Independence	Number	Share (%)	Cases
Yes	Yes	18	53	Albania, Bosnia and Herzegovina, Bulgaria, Croatia, Estonia, France, Georgia, Greece, Italy, Kosovo, Lithuania, Moldova, Montenegro, North Macedonia, Romania, Slovakia, Slovenia, Ukraine
No	Yes	8	23	Belgium, Denmark, Iceland, Ireland, Latvia, Malta, Netherlands, UK[*]
Yes	No	5	15	Poland, Portugal, Serbia, Spain, Turkey
No	No	3	9	Finland, Norway, Sweden

[*] The UK includes the different courts services for England and Wales, Scotland, and Northern Ireland

exceptions to this rule, adding up almost one quarter of the cases. Second, the model of independent judicial councils is by far the most frequent approach to judicial governance among the countries covered by the table. It is interesting, however, that this model exists in Italy, France, and in a number of Central and Eastern European countries (in Greece a weaker version of the judicial council exists). This reinforces the idea that this model—based mostly on the Italian experience—disseminated to countries in transition from authoritarian regimes to democracy in Central and Eastern Europe, aided by European institutions.[17] Without such dynamics of dissemination, this model, which is nowadays the most frequent approach to judicial governance in Europe, might have been an idiosyncratic trait of countries like Italy, France, and to some extent Greece.

Finally, there is one additional element to be taken into account. There are countries in the sample that have been classified as having an institutional design which makes their organs for judicial governance less independent from political actors: Poland, Portugal, Serbia, Spain, Turkey, Finland, Norway, and Sweden. But the variation within this group of countries is very sharp and has important consequences.

Such variation refers, first, to the type of organ for judicial governance, with some instances having a courts service and other ones having a judicial council. This is very relevant because the problems associated to political control over the organ of judicial governance are lower if powers over judicial careers are held by other institutions. To mention just one example, we can refer to the situation of judicial independence in Norway. This country is based on the courts service model, and politicians have a priori a say in the composition of this institution. But the powers over judicial careers of the Norwegian Courts Administration are not significant. A separate Judicial Appointments Board exists in this country, Norway, achieving very high levels of judicial independence.

The differences between countries in this group do not end with that. They also refer to the level of democratic quality of the countries and to the type of connections between political actors and the institutions of judicial governance, that create

---

[17] Bobek and Kosar (2014); Castillo-Ortiz (2019).

differences within groups of countries that have a priori similarities in their model of judicial governance. For instance, the members of the Spanish judicial council are appointed by the chambers of the Spanish Parliament, but the system requires a parliamentary majority of three-fifths for appointment. Thus, the procedure does not eliminate the connections between political actors and members of the institution, but minimizes the risk of single-party control of the judicial council. By contrast, the new system of appointment in Poland has a subtle but very important variation. Members of the Polish *Krajowa Rada Sądownictwa* are appointed by the Parliament by a three-fifths majority, but in case this threshold is not reached, a subsidiary simple majority can be used for the appointment.[18] This, in the words of Sadurski, 'gives the ruling party a decisive say in the composition of the KRS'.[19]

2.5 Ideal Types and Practical Examples

In the previous section, I identified four ideal types of organs for judicial governance defined by their range of powers and their independence vis-à-vis politicians. In this section, I provide a reflection on each of these types and present some practical examples of how they work in the real world. This analysis is provided while acknowledging that a wide variation exists within types.

2.5.1 Powerful and Formally Independent: The Hegemonic European Model

The first configuration in the Truth Table (Table 2.1) refers to institutions with powers over the careers of judges and a majority of whose members are appointed by actors other than politicians. The range of powers of these institutions varies, with some organs for judicial governance having more powers than others. But in general, all of these organs have sufficient competences over judicial careers as to be considered instances of the judicial council model.

Theoretically, these institutions should have a great advantage: being more powerful and independent, these organs for judicial governance have more capacity to protect judges from the political branches of government. But in exchange for this positive aspect, this institutional design comes with a number of risks. Among them, the possibility to exert great power without subjection to political accountability,

---

[18] Sadurski (2018) Bad Response to a Tragic Choice: the Case of Polish Council of the Judiciary. In: VerfBlog. https://verfassungsblog.de/bad-response-to-a-tragic-choice-the-case-of-polish-council-of-the-judiciary. Accessed 10 September 2022.
[19] Ibid.

which might lead to corporatism,[20] increasing influence over public policy and the judicialization of politics.[21]

Garuopa and Ginsburg describe how the cases of France and Italy, with strong councils insulated from political control, have given rise to debates or reforms in these countries around the need to increase the accountability of judges.[22] The idea of an unaccountable council is particularly worrying when it interacts with other factors, such as a judiciary socialized under authoritarian values. Guarneri summarizes the situation: 'as external independence increases, the likelihood also increases that courts will be more or less out of step with national political majorities. This fact can lead to serious tensions, especially in transitional or consolidating democracies, where the rule of law values are not always entrenched among the political class and the public and most judges have often been socialised in a non-democratic environment'.[23]

Some instances also show an additional problem: that formal designs of councils maximizing independence hide informal practices subjecting the institutions to political control. The experience of North Macedonia is interesting in this regard. The council in this country has followed the French-Italian approach but literature suggests the existence of problems with the *de facto* level of independence of the organ. Preshova et al. have argued that 'it is rather evident that the judiciary [of North Macedonia] was not ready for the high level of self-government'.[24] However, the analysis of the authors reveals that the problem in this country was not the excessive insulation of the North Macedonian judiciary, but rather precisely a failure in the mechanisms that should have ensured judicial independence. According to the authors, the problem in this country was one of 'undue political pressure from the executive and ruling party elites (…) extensive political pressure on the judiciary and judicial council, often through informal networks and means of political control (…) [including revealed] informal mechanisms of governmental and party control over the processes of recruitment, promotion and dismissal of judges, as well as governmental influence over high profile court verdicts'.[25] The North Macedonian council is a paradox: it was designed as a strong and independent council, but informal mechanisms of political control show what happens precisely when independence is lost.

---

[20] Solomon (2018), p. 44.
[21] Garoupa and Ginsburg (2009a, b), p. 61.
[22] Garoupa and Ginsburg (2009a, b), p. 108.
[23] Carlo Guarnieri (2013), p. 354.
[24] Preshova et al. (2017), p. 22.
[25] Ibid., pp. 22–23.

2.5.2 Independent and Managerial: The Standard Courts Service Model

The second configuration in Table 2.1 comprises institutions with limited powers over judicial careers and whose system of appointment includes at least half of its members not elected by political actors. These institutions have clear advantages. They are independent from political actors and, given their restricted range of powers, they have scarce possibilities to damage judicial independence themselves. The group includes institutions as diverse as the organs for judicial governance of the UK (including the separate organs for England and Wales, Scotland, and Northern Ireland), Denmark, Ireland, and Latvia, among others. Despite the diversity within this group, countries in this category generally have consolidated, high-quality democracies. It has been suggested that institutions for judicial governance have made in these countries a contribution to judicial independence.[26]

The similarities among these organs for judicial governance should not obscure their differences. Bunjevac's explanation of the contrast between the Irish courts service and the model in England and Wales is particularly illuminating.[27] The author labels the Irish model as based in a 'majority partnership' because judicial members constitute the voting majority in the board of the institution, while the model of England and Wales is called 'minority partnership' because judicial participation constitutes less than half of the board.[28] Furthermore, in the English and Welsh model, the Lord Chancellor—appointed at the advice of the prime minister and member of the Cabinet—and the Lord Chief Justice—the Head of the Judiciary, appointed by a panel convened by the Judicial Appointments Commission—retain significant powers, to the point that when the board of the Courts and Tribunals Service cannot reach agreement by consensus they must refer the issue to them for a decision.[29] The Lord Chancellor and the Lord Chief Justice also approve the appointment of the board members and save those holding ex officio positions. Given the details of its design and the more preeminent position of the Lord Chief Justice, the model has been classified as one of independent judicial governance, but it clearly retains traces of hybridity.[30]

The main risk for independent courts services has to do with a potential scenario of insertion into an illiberal political context. These organs seem to do well in a context of a functioning liberal democracy. But would they be able to protect judicial independence in a context of illiberal disregard for the rule of law? This points at the configurational nature of institutions. Similar institutions produce different results when interacting with different political and legal environments. The three UK courts services (for England and Wales, Scotland, and Northern Ireland), for

---

[26] Win Voermans (2003), p. 2141.
[27] Bunjevac (2020).
[28] Ibid., pp. 35–39.
[29] Ibid., p. 39.
[30] See also Castillo-Ortiz (2017).

instance, interact with a consolidated democracy in which there are formal and informal mechanisms to guarantee judicial independence. In the context of a liberal democracy, managerial institutions such as courts services can be useful organs. But a hypothesis is that those very institutions could become insufficient to protect judicial independence in countries with illiberal executives. The reason is that, deprived from powers over judicial careers, they would have little resistance to offer against authoritarian politicians. In such a context, the role and resilience of remaining institutions for judicial governance, such as judicial appointment organs, might become extraordinarily important.

2.5.3 Powerful but Politically Appointed: Politicized Judicial Councils

A third type of organ for judicial governance is featured by a wide range of powers over the careers of judges combined with *de jure* political control over the appointment of members. This type of council has an advantage: accountability—to politicians—is maximized in the design of the institution. In exchange for this 'advantage', these types of approaches can be problematic, because they run with the risk of undermining the independence of the organ for judicial governance.

A good example of organs in this category is provided by the Spanish case. The Spanish *Consejo General del Poder Judicial* is featured by a wide range of powers together with a system of parliamentary appointment of all its members. As a result, according to Íñiguez Hernández, it is the leaders of the political parties who choose according to their proportional parliamentary strength the composition of the institution.[31] The result, according to the author, is a Council scarcely effective vis-à-vis threats to independence from political actors.[32] Note that the design of the Spanish judicial council does not necessarily translate into a subjugated judiciary. In a country like Spain, judges still enjoy a wide range of guarantees of independence, from the system of recruitment to the tenure character of their positions.

Other cases in this category are notably more problematic. After all, the supermajority required for the appointment of members of the Spanish judicial council minimizes the risks of the institution being controlled by a single party. That is not the case of other instances in this category. As explained earlier, Poland has become a paradigmatic example of rule of law backsliding in Europe. Central to this process has been the control by the ruling party of the judicial council and the judiciary of the country.[33] In this country, the process of appointment of members of the council has been modified by the ruling Law and Justice (PiS) party. Initially, the majority of members of the council, 15 judges, were elected by peer judges. But after a legislation passed in December 2017, the council members are to be elected

---

[31] Íñiguez Hernández (2014), p. 149.
[32] Ibid., p. 149; Pérez (2018).
[33] Kovács and Scheppele (2018); Sadurski (2019).

by the parliament by a 3/5 majority and, in case this threshold is not reached, by a simple majority.[34] Given that the powers of the Polish judicial council are slightly more limited than those of some European counterparts, these manoeuvres intended at controlling the institution might seem surprising. Sadurski's work on the process of rule of law backsliding in Poland is useful to understand this apparent paradox. Albeit institutionally weaker than other European judicial councils, the powers of the *Krajowa Rada Sądownictwa* (KRS) still include the nomination of candidates for a judicial position. According to the author, 'PiS from the very beginning of its campaign against the judiciary considered the judicial component of the KRS to be the main obstacle to its reform'.[35]

2.5.4 The Residual Type: Managerial and Politically Appointed

A fourth type of organ for judicial governance is that of courts services, with little powers over the careers of judges, which are nonetheless formally under the control of political actors. This combination is not very frequent in the sample, and that might be for a reason: when organs for judicial governance have fewer powers 'different actors—including politicians—have fewer incentives to play battles over their control'.[36] The configuration covers organs such as those, Finland, Sweden, and Norway, countries which perform excellently in different indexes of democratic quality.

This category opens two interesting lines of inquiry. First, given the proximity of the Nordic countries covered by this type, it is not difficult to hypothesize that there might be some sort of cross-country observation that explains why Finland, Sweden and Norway (and only them) opted for this approach to judicial governance. The second has to do, again, with the capacity of institutions of this type to protect judicial independence in a—hypothetical—scenario of a country ruled by an executive of illiberal tendencies. In this case, the risk posed by the limited powers of the institution—as explained for the subtype of 'standard court services'—is complemented by the more political approach to the appointment of its members.

2.6 Powers, Independence, and Democratic Quality

Drawing on the information provided so far in this chapter, there are two issues that I would like to emphasize. The first of them is that organs for judicial governance

---

[34] Sadurski (2018), p. 39.
[35] Ibid., p. 38.
[36] Castillo-Ortiz (2017), p. 331.

are, with no exception, subject to inherent dilemmas of institutional design. The second is that, theoretically and a priori, the model of formally independent judicial councils seems well equipped when it comes to defending democracy and the rule of law against illiberal actors. This is because these institutions are designed to insulate judiciaries from political actors, protecting judicial independence and thus facilitating the role of courts systems as a constraint and a check on political power. This, however, contrasts with a fact: as shown in Fig. 2.1, countries following the model of independent judicial councils actually do not perform particularly well when it comes to democratic quality.

Figure 2.1 shows all the approaches to judicial governance explored so far in this book. It also shows the average score in the V-Dem liberal democracy index of the countries by model of judicial governance. The group with the highest average democratic quality is that of countries with a formally dependent courts service model. These countries exhibit a significantly higher average democratic quality than countries with an independent judicial council. Furthermore, countries with judicial councils—either *de jure* dependent or *de jure* independent—do not compare very well with the rest of the groups. Formally independent judicial councils have a significantly lower average democratic quality than both formally dependent and independent courts services. And the group of dependent judicial councils has one of the lowest average levels of democratic quality in the sample.

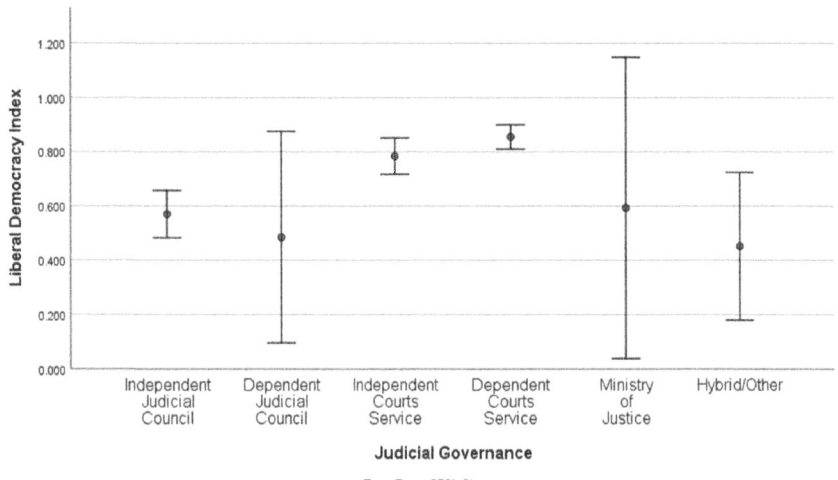

Fig. 2.1 Types of organs of judicial governance and democratic quality

2.7 Conclusion: Towards the Best Imperfect Model for Judicial Governance

This book explores the relationship between judicial governance and democracy. In this chapter, I have scrutinized the design of organs for judicial governance in Europe, analysing the trade-offs inherent in such institutional design. Precisely because these trade-offs are difficult to circumvent, designing good organs for judicial governance seems a difficult task. Judiciaries in liberal democracies are expected to display certain characteristics and to uphold a number of values. In designing organs for judicial governance, sometimes those values are in tension. On the one hand, democracy requires not only judicial independence but also judicial accountability. As stated by O'Donnell, 'The judiciary must be free of undue influences from executive, legislative and private interests, and if that is the case, the judiciary must not abuse its autonomy for the pursuit of narrowly defined corporate interests'.[37] However, in designing organs of judicial governance, we need to decide whether we want to create more independent but less politically accountable institutions or the other way around. On the other hand, democracy not only requires an independent judicial branch but also judges which are individually independent. In creating strong organs for judicial governance, the independence of the judiciary as a whole might increase vis-à-vis politicians, but such strong organs might undermine the independence of individual judges within the judiciary as a body.

Not all approaches to judicial governance necessarily make an equally good contribution to democracy. In theory, the model of powerful and formally independent judicial councils seems a priori very well-suited to these purposes. This is such because this type of institution is well equipped to protect the judiciary from the assault of authoritarian politicians. In accumulating powers over the judicial branch, powerful judicial councils take these powers away from the other branches of government. And in maximizing independence in their design, these councils become less amenable to political instrumentalization.

This expectation, that independent judicial councils are good at protecting democracy, is however subject to two caveats. First, the trade-offs inherent to judicial governance also affect these powerful and independent judicial councils. The second caveat is that the model of independent judicial councils does not seem to be correlated to higher levels of democratic quality (Fig. 2.1). This adds to the puzzle presented in Chap. 1 that showed that countries with judicial councils are in general associated to lower levels of democratic quality than countries with courts services. Overall, this forces us to confront a paradox: the model of independent judicial councils is theoretically particularly well equipped to protect democracy, but countries with this approach to judicial governance have in general democracies of worse quality. The next chapters provide a more detailed analysis of this paradox.

---

[37] O'Donnell (2004), p. 44.

References

Bobek M, Kosar D (2014) Global solutions, local damages: a critical study in judicial councils in central and Eastern Europe. Ger Law J 15:1257–1292

Bunjevac T (2020) Judicial Self-Governance in the New Millennium. Springer, Electronic

Burbank SB (2007) Judicial independence, judicial accountability and interbranch relations. Georgetown Law J 95:909–927

Guarnieri C (2013) Judicial independence in Europe: threat or resource for democracy? Representation 49:347–359

Castillo-Ortiz PJ (2017) Councils of the judiciary and judges' perceptions of respect to their independence in Europe. Hague J Rule Law 9:315–336. https://doi.org/10.1007/s40803-017-0061-2

Castillo-Ortiz P (2019) The politics of implementation of the judicial council model in Europe. Eur Polit Sci Rev 11:503–520. https://doi.org/10.1017/S1755773919000298

Contini F, Mohr R (2008) Reconciling independence and accountability in judicial systems. Utrecht Law Rev 3:26. https://doi.org/10.18352/ulr.46

Garoupa N, Ginsburg T (2009a) The comparative law and economics of judicial councils. Berkeley J Int Law 27:53–83. https://doi.org/10.15779/z383s9h

Garoupa N, Ginsburg T (2009b) Guarding the guardians: judicial councils and judicial independence. Am J Comp Law 57:103–134

Iñiguez Hernández D (2014) La reforma del Consejo General del Poder Judicial en España. Noticia de otra reforma fallida. Cuad Fund Man Giménez Abad 7:147–167

Kovács K, Scheppele KL (2018) The fragility of an independent judiciary: lessons from Hungary and Poland—and the European Union. Communist Post-Communist Stud 51:189–200. https://doi.org/10.1016/j.postcomstud.2018.07.005

Larkins CM (1996) Judicial independence and democratization: a theoretical and conceptual analysis. Am J Comp Law 44:605–626. https://doi.org/10.2307/840623

O'Donnell G (2004) Why the rule of law matters. J Democr 15:32–46

Pérez AT (2018) Judicial self-government and judicial independence: the political capture of the general council of the judiciary in Spain. Ger Law J 19:1769–1800. https://doi.org/10.1017/S2071832200023233

Preshova D, Damjanovski I, Nechev Z (2017) The effectiveness of the 'European Model' of judicial independence in the western Balkans: judicial councils as a solution or a new cause of concern for judicial reforms, 2017/1.

Sadurski W (2019) Poland's constitutional breakdown. Oxford University Press

Sadurski W (2018) How democracy dies (in Poland): a case study of anti-constitutional populist backsliding. Syd Law Sch - Leg Stud Res Pap 18:1–70

Solomon PH (2018) Transparency in the work of judicial councils: the experience of (East) European Countries. Rev Cent East Eur Law 43:43–62. https://doi.org/10.1163/15730352-04301003

van Dijk F (2021) Perceptions of the Independence of Judges in Europe Congruence of Society and Judiciary. Palgrave, Electronic

Voigt S (2021) Mind the gap: analyzing the divergence between constitutional text and constitutional reality. Int J Const Law 19:1778–1809

Voermans W (2003) Councils for the judiciary in Europe: trends and models. In: Fernández Segado F (ed) The Spanish constitution in the European constitutional context. Dykinson, Madrid, pp 2133–2144

Open Access This chapter is licensed under the terms of the Creative Commons Attribution 4.0 International License (http://creativecommons.org/licenses/by/4.0/), which permits use, sharing, adaptation, distribution and reproduction in any medium or format, as long as you give appropriate credit to the original author(s) and the source, provide a link to the Creative Commons license and indicate if changes were made.

The images or other third party material in this chapter are included in the chapter's Creative Commons license, unless indicated otherwise in a credit line to the material. If material is not included in the chapter's Creative Commons license and your intended use is not permitted by statutory regulation or exceeds the permitted use, you will need to obtain permission directly from the copyright holder.

Chapter 3
Modernization, Democracy, and Judicial Governance

3.1 Introduction

In Chap. 2, I presented different models of organs for judicial governance, analysing their respective advantages and disadvantages.

A priori, courts services can be compatible with liberal institutions and perform an efficient role in the context of a well-functioning democracy. However, in countries relying on this model of judicial governance, judicial independence is protected through arrangements that go beyond the courts service, such as independent judicial appointment commissions. If these alternative arrangements were to fail in protecting the judicial branch vis-à-vis a potential illiberal or authoritarian executive, the courts service might be able to do little to protect judicial independence, thus posing a risk for the stability of democracy.

Strong judicial councils seem theoretically equally dangerous when they are controlled by politicians, at least if they are under the control of one single political party. This is because this party could instrumentalize the council, for instance, putting it at the service of the government and against the opposition. Politically controlled councils are likely to be unable to maximize the value of judicial independence. As put by Garoupa and Ginsburg, 'Sometimes these pressures for more accountability can lead to assaults on judicial independence, particularly if a small group of principals is able to control the process of supervision. In such circumstances, a politically accountable, strong judiciary may revert back to a politically dependent, weak judiciary, in a rising authoritarian regime'.[1]

The remaining model is that of strong and (formally) independent councils. A priori, this model of judicial governance can safeguard judicial independence to a large extent, and therefore, it seems a very *garantiste* option in terms of its contribution to the preservation of liberal democracies. However, empirical data seems to show reasons for scepticism. My analyses showed that the quality of democracy in countries that had implemented this type of independent judicial council was not

---

[1] Garoupa and Ginsburg (2009a, b), p. 61.

particularly high compared to countries with other models of judicial governance, but rather the opposite.

This chapter puts these findings in context. In particular, the chapter uses statistical techniques to shed light on the paradoxical relationship between judicial governance and democracy at which my previous analyses hinted. My findings suggest that, when more factors are taken into account, there is no evidence to fear that judicial councils are actually detrimental to democratic quality.

More specifically my work in this chapter is grounded in modernization theory, which posits that political democratization is associated with economic development.[2] Countries often implemented judicial councils during processes of transition to democracy. These countries had often younger and more fragile democratic systems of government. In this chapter, I show that at similar levels of economic development, countries with an independent judicial council do not do worse in terms of democratic quality after all. In the most conservative reading, the data qualifies the evidence presented in Chaps. 1 and 2 about the poor performance of judicial councils with regards to democratic quality.

This finding has important policy implications that will be discussed in more detail in Chap. 5.

3.2 The Political Origins of Organs for Judicial Governance

In Chap. 1, I explained that different European countries have opted for different models of judicial governance. Drawing on Bobek and Kosar,[3] these models were classified into some ideal types: the judicial council model, the courts service model, and the Ministry of Justice model. With this background, an obvious question arises: which factors explain this variation across countries? Or said in different terms, which reasons explain these different choices of models of judicial governance in Europe?

Despite theoretical and empirical differences among authors, most literature in the field seems to agree on certain factors as to the explanation behind the diversity of approaches to judicial governance in Europe. These factors are as follows:

- *Authoritarian backgrounds and democratization.* This is one of the most frequently used variables in the literature. Works in the field have systematically found evidence about the impact of levels of democracy and authoritarian backgrounds in choices of models of judicial governance.[4] In general, it is expected that countries that have undergone—and are exiting—authoritarian periods will implement the judicial council model as a way to signal commitment to democracy once authoritarianism is over, and to try to stabilize their young political systems.

---

[2] See for a recent account Inglehart (2018), p. 116 ff.

[3] Bobek and Kosar (2014).

[4] Castillo-Ortiz (2019); Garoupa and Ginsburg (2015), p. 132; Garoupa and Ginsburg (2009a, b), p. 58; Tin Bunjevac (2017), pp. 822–823.

- *Legal families.* Evidence about the impact on judicial governance of types of legal families is mixed in the literature. On the one hand, in their important work on this topic, Garoupa and Ginsburg did not find evidence about the capacity of legal families to explain the implementation of systems of judicial governance.[5] In previous research, however, it was found that having a Romanistic legal family could be part of the explanation for why certain countries implemented a judicial council model.[6] The idea behind the impact of legal families on choices of models of judicial governance has to do with the processes of diffusion and imitation among countries with similar characteristics, and with more easy adaptation of certain models of judicial governance to the underlying characteristics of diverse legal cultures.[7]
- *Europeanization.* Finally, different authors have argued that the diffusion of the judicial council model in Europe had to do with Europeanizing pressures: its implementation seemed to become a 'soft standard' for many countries that aimed at accession to the European Union, this being the case especially for Central and Eastern European countries.[8] However, we know less about how these Europeanizing dynamics have impacted the diffusion and survival of the other approaches to judicial governance in Europe.

Let me focus on the first set of variables presented above: authoritarian backgrounds and dynamics of democratization. As explained earlier, this set of explanatory variables is particularly relevant to my argument, as the main object of this book is the study of the relationship between judicial governance and democracy. Furthermore, in Chapter 1, I showed that a somewhat paradoxical correlation existed between democratic quality and judicial governance: countries relying on the courts service model tend to have a better quality of democracy than countries adopting the judicial council model. The analyses in Table 3.1 can help to explain why.

The first column in Table 3.1 confirms that there seems to be a tendency according to which higher liberal democracy scores are associated with the existence of the courts service model; countries with high liberal democracy scores are also less likely to have a judicial council, although the association is not significant. Additionally, for the sample, countries with a Ministry of Justice model seem to be positively associated with a higher democratic quality, although the association is rather weak.

The second column in Table 3.1 provides further information that can be useful to make sense of the puzzling relationship between judicial governance and democracy. It shows that countries that have a long, uninterrupted history of democratic quality are associated with the courts service model and countries that experienced authoritarian breakdowns are associated with the judicial council model, with the

---

[5] Garoupa and Ginsburg (2015), p. 133.

[6] Castillo-Ortiz (2019).

[7] Ibid., pp. 4–5; Daniela Piana (2009), pp. 818–819; Garoupa and Ginsburg (2009a, b), p. 112.

[8] Bobek and Kosar (2014); Castillo-Ortiz (2019); Daniela Piana (2009); Denis Preshova et al., *The Effectiveness of the 'European Model' of Judicial Independence in the Western Balkans: Judicial Councils as a Solution or a New Cause of Concern for Judicial Reforms*, 2017/1, 2017; Garoupa and Ginsburg (2015), p. 128.

Table 3.1 Correlations (Spearman's Rho) between models of governance and political background[9]

		Current liberal democracy	Historic liberal democracy	Reinstated constitution
Judicial council	Correlation coefficient	−0.274	−0.349*	−0.421**
	Sig. (2-tailed)	0.066	0.017	0.006
	N	46	46	41
Courts service	Correlation coefficient	0.409*	0.459**	0.623**
	Sig. (2-tailed)	0.005	0.001	0.000
	N	46	46	41
Ministry of justice	Correlation coefficient	0.063	−0.108	0.129
	Sig. (2-tailed)	0.676	0.476	0.423
	N	46	46	41
Hybrid/other	Correlation coefficient	−0.147	0.024	−0.169
	Sig. (2-tailed)	0.331	0.874	0.291
	N	46	46	41

** Correlation is significant at the 0.01 level (2-tailed)
* Correlation is significant at the 0.05 level (2-tailed)

correlations being significant in both cases. The correlations support with empirical evidence the idea that judicial councils were an arrangement created in democratic transitions. There might be many reasons for this. By way of hypothesis, it might be that countries experiencing authoritarian traumas believed that judicial councils would help stabilize their young democracies. It might also be that these countries wanted to signal a commitment to democracy through the creation of judicial councils in the transition period, or that they imitated successful experiences of democratic transition in other countries. Whatever the reason, the fact that there is a clear association between authoritarian backgrounds and implementation of judicial councils can help us understand the paradox that was formulated in Chap. 1: perhaps countries with a judicial council have lower levels of democratic quality precisely because these institutions were created in young, fragile democracies. Later in this chapter, I explore this question in more detail.

---

[9] To account for 'current liberal democracy' status and for 'historically liberal democracy', I use the V-Dem v.11 liberal democracy index ('v2x_libdem'), countries being classed as authoritarian if in a given year they score less than 0.5 in this variable, and not authoritarian otherwise. For 'historically liberal democracy' countries score 1 if democratic for at least 90 consecutive years. For the variable 'preserved/reinstated pre-authoritarian constitution', I exclude the countries that were historical liberal democracies, and I use the Comparative Constitutions Project as my main source Elkins and Ginsburg (2021) Characteristics of National Constitutions, Version 3.0.

The last column in Table 3.1 also tells us something very interesting about democratization, transition periods, and judicial governance. As seen above, countries that have experienced a repressive regime generally tend to implement a judicial council once they democratize. However, there is a caveat to this: the mechanism seems to depend on whether the country enacts a new constitution in the transition period or instead returns to the constitution that existed prior to the repressive regime. Countries with an authoritarian past but which preserved or reinstated their pre-authoritarian constitution at the end of the repressive regime are generally associated with courts service model. This finding sits in line with previous research in the field,[10] confirming that constitutional politics in the transition period had a very important impact on choices regarding models of judicial governance.

A final observation has to do with the implications of the association between authoritarian backgrounds and the implementation of the judicial council model. This correlation suggests that European countries have generally taken a reactive approach to the implementation of this approach to judicial governance. It is generally when they have experienced authoritarian regimes, and as a response to this, that the judicial council model is implemented. This approach seems to have been reinforced by European institutions, that only insisted on the need to create judicial councils in younger democracies, as opposed to older democracies.[11] This seemed to be the case of Central and Eastern European countries. On the one hand, these countries had authoritarian regimes. On the other hand, their democratic transitions took place when the judicial council had already become a standard of good practice promoted by European institutions.[12] These two factors converged in these instances, facilitating the case for the implementation of judicial councils.[13] The question is whether these institutions lived up to their promise of protection of democracy.

3.3 Modernization, Democracy, and Judicial Governance

Empirical research in political science has tried to understand the causes that explain the creation and consolidation of democratic systems of government. The most successful approach so far to this fascinating question is modernization theory.

Modernization theory poses that processes of democratization are strongly linked to economic development. Already in 1959, Lipset presented evidence about this link between economic development and democracy, and tried to explain its causal mechanisms. In the words of the author, 'the factors of industrialization, urbanization, wealth and education are so closely interrelated as to form one common factor. And the factors subsumed under economic development carry with it the political

---

[10] Castillo-Ortiz (2019).
[11] Bobek and Kosar (2014).
[12] Ibid.
[13] Castillo-Ortiz (2019).

correlate of democracy'.[14] Thus, the causal link between economic development and democratization is the process of modernization.

Subsequent research has deepened and fine-tuned our understanding of the relationship between economic development and democracy, focusing on changes to class structures and societal values. As put by Inglehart[15] 'economic development brings democracy *if* it changes people's values and behaviour. Economic development is conducive to democratization insofar as it (1) creates a large and articulate middle class and (2) transforms people's values and motivations, so that they give higher priority to free choice and freedom of expression'.

In their more recent work, Norris and Inglehart point to four mechanisms linking economic development and democratization.[16] First, urbanization and industrialization facilitate political communication and organization. Second, when economic survival is guaranteed, people give self-expression values a higher priority. Third, educational levels help people become more 'effective at getting democracy'. Fourth, the increasing importance of the knowledge sector translates into more people having jobs that require 'thinking for themselves'. Additionally, the authors point at democracy's big advantage: 'it provides a non-violent way to replace a country's leaders'.[17]

This connection between economic development and democratization can be enlightening with regards to the paradoxical relations between judicial governance and democratic quality that I am scrutinizing in this book. Strong, independent judicial councils were a priori designed in such a way that they should make a contribution to the quality of democracy in the countries where they are implemented. However, as I explained in the previous chapters, countries with such institutions fare worse with regards to democratic quality.

My expectation is that modernization theory can shed light on this paradox. In particular, countries with strong and independent judicial councils are also countries where the background conditions that lead to democratization, such as economic development, are less present. Therefore, if we take into account the effects of socio-economic backgrounds which are less favourable to democratization in countries with judicial councils, we might have to reassess the associations of these institutions with democratic quality. Overall, my hypothesis in this chapter is that the existence of judicial councils is actually *not* associated with lower democratic quality when the level of economic development of the country is accounted for. The analyses in this chapter are thus not intended at establishing causation, but simply at discarding a certain association between my variables.

---

[14] Lipset (1959), p. 80.
[15] Inglehart (2018), p. 117.
[16] Norris and Inglehart (2019), p. 411.
[17] Ibid., p. 411.

3.4 Methods

My aim in this chapter, which is central to the argument of the book, is to shed further light on the relationship between judicial governance and democracy. In particular, I want to better understand the relationship between democratic quality and the two variables related to judicial governance covered in the previous chapters: the type of model of judicial governance, and the level of *de jure* independence of such a model. However, I do this by taking into account at least one additional factor: the level of economic development of the countries in my sample, which according to modernization theory should be a major explanatory variable of democratic quality.

In order to carry out my analysis, I used statistics, and in particular robust regressions. These allowed the assessment of the net association between the quality of democracy and the existence of certain institutional arrangements (such as a judicial council) in the countries of the sample. The analyses does so while 'discounting' the impact of my control variable, the GDP per capita of each country, which I used to measure economic development. The objective is to understand the correlation between judicial governance and democratic quality once the impact of economic development is controlled for.

Robust regressions are a very useful tool to understand net associations. However, like any methodological tool they also have some limitations. The most important for the purposes of this research is that, in order to introduce many explanatory variables in the model (to 'control' for many variables), it is a good practice to have a high number of cases in the sample. This was not the case with the database that I am using, which included fewer than 50 cases. For that reason, I took a cautious approach and never included simultaneously more than two independent variables in the models.

This, in turn, meant that I had to seek other strategies of research design in order to understand how other factors might have a role in the relationship between judicial governance and democracy that I am studying here. In particular, different operationalizations of the phenomena permitted an understanding of different aspects of the object of study while still using robust regressions. In this regard, I ran different analyses for judicial councils in general, courts services in general, formally independent judicial councils specifically, and judicial councils a majority of whose members are politically appointed. For each of these, I ran a different robust regression, which allowed me to understand how different designs of the models of judicial governance relate to democracy when economic development is accounted for. My expectation was that the analyses in this chapter will point at the negative association between judicial councils and democratic quality disappearing when economic development is controlled for.

All the analyses carried out in this chapter are robust regressions.[18] In all cases, I test the impact of different approaches to judicial governance on democratic quality.

---

[18] For all analyses (Tables 3.2, 3.3, 3.4, and 3.5), the original approach was the use of linear regressions. However, the analyses did not meet the assumption of heteroscedasticity, so I finally opted for robust regressions. Also, for all the analyses (Tables 3.2, 3.3, 3.4, and 3.5), I use the Gross Domestic Product per capita (at purchasing power parity). In all cases, the variable is transformed

Table 3.2 Judicial councils and quality of democracy (robust regressions)

	Liberal democracy index	Electoral democracy index	Equality before law index
(Intercept)	−1.77* (0.71)	−0.84 (0.43)	−0.08 (0.23)
logGDP	0.24*** (0.07)	0.16*** (0.04)	0.10*** (0.02)
Judicial council	−0.03 (0.07)	−0.02 (0.04)	−0.02 (0.02)
R^2	0.42	0.31	0.30
Num. obs	46	46	46
RMSE	0.11	0.08	0.05

*** $p < 0.001$; * $p < 0.01$; * $p < 0.05$

Table 3.3 Courts services and quality of democracy (robust regressions)

	Liberal democracy index	Electoral democracy index	Equality before law index
(Intercept)	−1.83*** (0.49)	−0.93*** (0.25)	−0.15 (0.23)
logGDP	0.24*** (0.05)	0.16*** (0.02)	0.10*** (0.02)
Cservice	0.04 (0.06)	0.02 (0.03)	0.02 (0.02)
R^2	0.43	0.34	0.30
Num. obs	46	46	46
RMSE	0.12	0.09	0.05

*** $p < 0.001$; * $p < 0.01$; * $p < 0.05$

In all cases, I do this while controlling for the GDP per capita of the country in 2020.[19] My dependent variables are always three different proxies to the quality of democracy in a country: the Liberal Democracy Index, the Electoral Democracy Index, and the Equality Before the Law and Individual Liberties Index from the V-Dem project (version 11).

I have opted for using these three different proxies in order to guarantee the reliability of the analyses. Each of these indexes has advantages and disadvantages, which are explained below.

- The Liberal Democracy Index is a very comprehensive proxy to democratic quality, which takes into account not only aspects related to the electoral dynamics

---

using a logarithmic function. The key independent variable (models of judicial governance) follows the scores justified in Appendix 1.

[19] World Bank, Our World in Data (2020) GDP per capita, 2020.

3.4 Methods

Table 3.4 Independent councils and quality of democracy (robust regressions)

	Liberal democracy index	Electoral democracy index	Equality before law index
(Intercept)	−1.95*** (0.40)	−0.82* (0.30)	−0.14 (0.23)
logGDP	0.25*** (0.04)	0.16*** (0.03)	0.10*** (0.02)
Independent judicial council	−0.00 (0.04)	−0.03 (0.03)	−0.01 (0.02)
R^2	0.42	0.34	0.29
Num. obs	46	46	46
RMSE	0.12	0.09	0.05

*** $p < 0.001$; ** $p < 0.01$; * $p < 0.05$

Table 3.5 Politically dependent councils and quality of democracy (robust regressions)

	Liberal democracy index	Electoral democracy index	Equality before law index
(Intercept)	−2.00*** (0.35)	−0.98*** (0.20)	−0.18 (0.18)
logGDP	0.26*** (0.03)	0.17*** (0.02)	0.10*** (0.02)
Dependent judicial councils	−0.06 (0.08)	0.09 (0.05)	−0.01 (0.03)
R^2	0.41	0.31	0.27
Num. obs	46	46	46
RMSE	0.11	0.08	0.05

*** $p < 0.001$; ** $p < 0.01$; * $p < 0.05$

of the countries but also checks on power and the rule of law. However, this index is constructed taking into account, inter alia, aspects such as judicial independence in each country. As a result, the main disadvantage of this index is the risk of an endogenous relationship between the independent and the dependent variable.
- To account for the problem presented above, I replicated all my analyses using the Electoral Democracy Index, which is less complete—as it is focused on electoral aspects—but excludes the possibility of a problem of endogeneity in the analyses. This index measures aspects such as electoral competition, freedom for political and civil society organizations, fairness of elections, existence of freedom of expression, and an independent media.[20]
- Finally, to reinforce the analyses, I also used the Equality before the Law and Individual Freedoms Index. Such index does not capture the dynamics of electoral competition in the countries of the sample. It also does not include indicators of

---

[20] Coppedge et al. (2021) V-Dem Codebook v.11.1, p. 44.

judicial independence (only access to justice for men and women), removing also the risk of endogeneity that might impact the Liberal Democracy Index. It is thus a much less complete proxy to democratic quality, and so it should be considered just as an additional test for the analyses carried out.

While none of the three indexes is perfect, together the three of them can offer some insights into the relationship between judicial governance and democracy in the sample. In the next section, the analyses are presented.

3.5 Judicial Governance and Democratic Quality: A Statistical Approach

Table 3.2 shows the correlation between the judicial council model and the different indicators of democratic quality, when controlling for the GDP of the countries. As can be seen, in all cases the models (as per the R Squared) can explain between 30 and 42 per cent of the variation in the phenomena explored. The GDP of the country was very strongly correlated with democratic quality. As predicted by modernization theory, GDP is strongly correlated to democratic quality in all three indicators. More importantly, the effect of having a judicial council on the quality of democracy is not statistically significant.

In Chap. 1, I discussed evidence suggesting that countries with a judicial council have a worse level of democratic quality. Table 3.2 strongly qualifies that information. It suggests that once we 'discount' the effect of economic development, there is no evidence to support the idea that judicial councils are detrimental to democratic quality. The finding is thus relevant, as it can help discard a potential powerful reason to reject the implementation of these institutions.

Table 3.3 complements this information by replicating the analyses for the main competing model: courts service institutions. The analyses confirmed the strong association between the GDP and the levels of democratic quality for all proxies. With regards to the courts service model, again, a substantively and statistically insignificant association was obtained.

Earlier in this book it was shown that judicial councils were associated with lower levels of democratic quality. But generally speaking, the analyses in Tables 3.2 and 3.3 suggest that there is no evidence to think that the judicial council model is bad for democratic quality, or to think that the courts service is good for it: once GDP is controlled for, the correlations between these models of judicial governance and democracy are insignificant.

Judicial councils, thus, do not seem to be a bad arrangement for democratic political systems. However, as I explained in Chap. 2, we can divide these institutions for judicial governance into two main types, depending on whether political actors have a protagonist role in the appointment of their members or not. In Tables 3.4 and 3.5, I analyse separately the correlation with democratic quality of formally independent and dependent judicial councils. I keep the GDP per capita as my control variable, because I believe that the background socio-economic conditions of each country are still relevant to these analyses.

As shown in Table 3.4, the association between judicial councils and democratic quality continues to be insignificant even when we take into account only those judicial councils for which at least half of their members are not appointed by political actors. Furthermore, something similar happens with those judicial councils for which more than half of their members are appointed by political actors (Table 3.5).

The findings in the analyses presented in Tables 3.2, 3.3, 3.4, and 3.5 are thus mixed news for judicial councils. The worst possible scenario for these institutions might have been evidence supporting the correlations found earlier in this book, according to which judicial councils were negatively correlated with democratic quality. This did not happen, and no evidence was found in such direction. But judicial councils were not positively correlated to democratic quality either. Not even when only taking into account those judicial councils that were more politically independent. Instead, at equal levels of economic development (measured by the GDP per capita), no significant correlations were found between any model of judicial governance and any index of democratic quality.

3.6 Conclusion

The associations presented in Chaps. 1 and 2 were somehow surprising. Judicial councils have become a 'soft' standard in Europe, but countries that have implemented these institutions fare worse in terms of democratic quality. What if, then, judicial councils were weakening after all the democracies that they were supposed to strengthen?

This chapter suggests that there is no reason for concern. It is a fact that European countries with a judicial council have, on average, democracies of worse quality. But judicial councils are not responsible for this. The interpretation of the analyses in this chapter suggests that such association is spurious, and that it can be better understood if we take into account extra-judicial factors such as the level of economic development of the countries. In modernization theory, economic development is associated with democratization. And in the countries of the sample, those with a judicial council happened to have, on average, lower levels of economic development. Said in other terms, modernization theory seems to explain the different levels of democratic quality that earlier were found as correlating with variation in models of judicial governance. And if the levels of economic development were the same for all countries—that is, *ceteris paribus*—then having a judicial council would not be associated with a lower level of democratic quality, nor to a higher one.

A final note in this chapter has to do with the tense relationship between *de jure* and *de facto* institutional independence. Some literature has recently analysed this relationship. For instance, Tsereteli showed how practices such as judicial recruitment can undermine *de jure* rules formally protecting judicial independence.[21] In

---

[21] Tsereteli (2020).

their work, Gutmann and Voigt found a negative association between *de jure* and *de facto* judicial independence, which seemed to be explained by cultural factors such as individualism and trust.[22] The authors suggest that it will be difficult to increase *de facto* judicial independence through *de jure* reforms. Something similar occurs with the relationship between *de jure* regulations of judicial governance and democratic quality, as evidenced in this chapter. Individually considered, the former does not seem to have significant general association to the latter. This being said, the picture is more complicated when we look at specific cases and the combination of *de jure* regulations of judicial governance with other factors. The next chapter analyses this in detail.

References

Bobek M, Kosar D (2014) Global solutions, local damages: a critical study in judicial councils in central and Eastern Europe. Ger Law J 15:1257–1292
Bunjevac T (2017) From individual judge to judicial bureaucracy: the emergence of judicial councils and the changing nature of judicial accountability in court administration. Univ New South Wales Law J 40:806–841
Castillo-Ortiz P (2019) The politics of implementation of the judicial council model in Europe. Eur Polit Sci Rev 11:503–520. https://doi.org/10.1017/S1755773919000298
Coppedge M, Gerring J, Knutsen CH, et al (2021) V-Dem Codebook v.11.1
Elkins Z, Ginsburg T (2021) Characteristics of National Constitutions, Version 3.0
Garoupa N, Ginsburg T (2009a) The comparative law and economics of judicial councils. Berkeley J Int Law 27:53–83. https://doi.org/10.15779/z383s9h
Garoupa N, Ginsburg T (2015) Judicial Reputation: A Comparative Theory. The University of Chicago Press
Garoupa N, Ginsburg T (2009b) Guarding the guardians: judicial councils and judicial independence. Am J Comp Law 57:103–134
Gutmann J, Voigt S (2020) Judicial independence in the EU: a puzzle. Eur J L Eco 49:83–100
Inglehart R (2018) Cultural evolution. Cambridge University Press, UK
Lipset SM (1959) Some social requisites of democracy: economic development and political legitimacy. Am Polit Sci Rev 53:69–105. https://doi.org/10.2307/1951731
Norris P, Inglehart R (2019) Cultural backlash. Cambridge University Press, UK/US/Australia/India/Singapure
Piana D (2009) The power knocks at the courts' back door: two waves of postcommunist judicial reforms. Comp Polit Stud 42:816–840
Tsereteli N (2020) Judicial recruitment in post-communist context: informal dynamics and façade reforms. Int J Leg Prof. https://doi.org/10.1080/09695958.2020.1776128

---

[22] Gutmann and Voigt (2020).

Open Access This chapter is licensed under the terms of the Creative Commons Attribution 4.0 International License (http://creativecommons.org/licenses/by/4.0/), which permits use, sharing, adaptation, distribution and reproduction in any medium or format, as long as you give appropriate credit to the original author(s) and the source, provide a link to the Creative Commons license and indicate if changes were made.

The images or other third party material in this chapter are included in the chapter's Creative Commons license, unless indicated otherwise in a credit line to the material. If material is not included in the chapter's Creative Commons license and your intended use is not permitted by statutory regulation or exceeds the permitted use, you will need to obtain permission directly from the copyright holder.

Chapter 4
Independent Judicial Councils and Democratic Quality: A Set-Theoretical Approach

4.1 Introduction

Chapter 3 of this book sought regression techniques to try to shed light on the connection between judicial governance arrangements and democratic quality. The analysis did not point to any significant evidence that differences in models of judicial governance were correlated with democratic quality. However, given the methodological tools used, the analysis was based on two epistemological assumptions. First, the analysis aimed at finding out the general association between judicial governance on democratic quality; but this might have hidden the role played by judicial governance in specific cases. Second, the analyses in the previous chapter tried to isolate the effect of the association between judicial governance and democratic quality from the effect of another variable—the GDP of the countries—instead of understanding how it interacts with a range of other factors.

To account for these two caveats and to complement the analyses carried out so far, this chapter uses a different technique: Qualitative Comparative Analysis (QCA). More particularly, the aim of this chapter is to try to understand the relationship of a specific institution of judicial governance—the model of judicial councils with *de jure* apolitical forms of appointment of members—with democratic quality. I focus on this model of judicial governance for two reasons. First, because it is the most frequent model in my sample of cases. Second, because it has been frequently deemed as a good standard of judicial governance, and thus a large part of the debate on this topic gravitates around this model.

In this chapter, I will try to find out whether the presence of the model of independent judicial councils is a logically necessary or sufficient condition for different levels of democratic quality. I will do so by including in my analysis other economic, political, and institutional conditions that might be relevant for the outcome.

The analyses do not contradict the findings of Chap. 3. On the contrary, as I will show, both regression techniques and QCA analyses can shed light on different but complementary aspects of the phenomenon explored.

4.2 Modernization, New Institutionalism, and the Role of Judiciaries in Democratic Quality. Theory and Configurational Hypotheses

Earlier in this book, I showed that countries with judicial councils do not perform particularly well when it comes to democratic quality. However, in Chap. 3, and using modernization theory, I hypothesized that this phenomenon might be masking an omitted variable bias: different levels of economic development are strongly correlated with both having certain models of judicial governance and also with having certain levels of democratic quality. The reason why countries with judicial councils had lower levels of democratic quality was, thus, not their model of judicial governance. It was, instead, that they tended to have a lower level of economic development.

The analyses in Chap. 3, however, presented an incomplete landscape, as they did not account for other factors beyond judicial governance and GDP. This chapter presents an analysis that includes a wider range of conditions, including EU membership and other judicial-institutional factors. Drawing on new institutionalist theory and modernization approaches, this section theorizes the relationship between these factors and democratic quality.

Political and economic background factors favouring democratic quality

In this chapter, I analyse the role of two background factors that can play a positive role in fostering democratic quality: economic development and EU membership.

Regarding economic development, much has been already said in Chap. 3 about the way in which modernization theory explains its relationship with democracy. A body of literature, starting with the work of Lipset, has shown significant evidence that economic development has a positive impact on democratization.[1] Inglehart suggests that the causal mechanism is linked to the way in which economic development fosters the creation of a middle class, as well as value and behavioural change, with an increasing emphasis on self-expression values.[2] The evidence presented in the previous chapter seemed to back this idea for the countries of the sample. In my QCA analyses in this chapter, thus, economic development is also included in the analyses.

In addition, in this chapter, I also consider another background condition of a political character: EU membership. This condition could be relevant for democratic quality for two reasons. First, because accession to the EU involves the requirement to meet certain democratic standards in the first place. Evidence in the field suggests that a realistic perspective of accession does indeed have a positive impact on democratic standards of candidate countries.[3] Second, it could be thought that membership of the EU should theoretically put constraints on authoritarian leaders of member states.

---

[1] Lipset (1959).
[2] Inglehart (2018), p. 117.
[3] Schimmelfennig and Scholtz (2008).

This second argument is, however, weaker, given the evidence in the literature about the inability of the EU to prevent rule of law backsliding in countries such as Poland or Hungary,[4] although it can be hypothesized that the total absence of EU membership would further free illiberal executives from constraints on their agendas.

New institutionalism and the role of institutions

Institutional explanations are a complement to the economic and political conditions presented above. In this chapter, I test three conditions related to institutions: the existence of an judicial council with a *de jure* apolitical form of appointment of its members, the level of judicial independence of the higher courts of the system, and the level of judicial corruption. These three questions shape institutions related to the judiciary in each country and can be relevant to understand their levels of democratic quality.

Literature in Judicial Politics approaches the relationship between judicial independence and democracy in different ways. A good part of the literature has shown evidence that democracy, and in particular party competition, leads to higher judicial independence.[5] Popova, however, provides a caveat in her very interesting explanation of judicial independence in emerging democracies. Her strategic pressure theory posited that 'in emerging democracies political competition hinders rather than promotes judicial independence'.[6] At the same time, another branch of literature has focused on the opposite phenomenon: how judicial independence matters for democratic quality. This idea is backed by the recent empirical research by Laebens and Lührmann,[7] which shows that independent judiciaries can aid in halting democratic erosion. Similarly, Gible and Randazzo found evidence that independent judiciaries played a positive role in preventing authoritarian change, albeit their work suggests that newly formed courts were more likely to suffer regime collapses.[8]

Democracy involves the existence of regular elections in which incumbents can be ousted. Institutions that govern the judicial branch or that are part of them can play a role in the quality of electoral democracy, and new institutionalism can explain why. According to new institutionalism, institutions explain the behaviour of political actors. In particular, rational choice new institutionalism argues that institutions pose constraints and incentives to political actors: when they seek to achieve their goals, they will take into account those incentives and constraints and modulate their behaviour accordingly.[9] Institutions are part of that system of incentives and constraints. In particular, the existence of an independent, functional judiciary can prevent political actors from undermining the quality of democracy in order to fraudulently achieve or maintain power. A more sociological approach to new institutionalism can also help explain the relationship of the institutions that govern or that are

---

[4] Pech and Scheppele (2017).
[5] See some recent discussions in Randazzo et al. (2016); Epperly (2019).
[6] Popova (2012).
[7] Laebens and Lührmann (2021).
[8] Gibler and Randazzo (2011).
[9] See Hall and Taylor (1996), pp. 944–945.

part of the judicial branch with democratic quality. As Larkins puts it, 'Once state actors learn not to transgress the legal bounds of the system to attain political goals, a constitutional culture will be attained, and lead to the consolidation of democratic rule. The courts can have a significant role in establishing this culture of legality if they are given adequate latitude to enact neutral justice, regulate the legality of government behaviour, and mandate important legal and constitutional values'.[10]

At a very basic level, a functional judicial branch can sanction a political actor willing to achieve or remain in power illegitimately. In anticipating such sanctions, political actors will abide by the rules of the game. However, democratic deconsolidation can happen more subtly, by tilting the electoral playing-field in favour of a political faction—usually the one in power. An independent, functional court system can prevent politicians from subtly manipulating the rules of party competition in their favour.

Thus, institutions matter. And judiciaries are an important part of the institutional framework in which parties and politicians operate. As said above, in this chapter, I analyse three important elements of conditions related to the court system:

a. First, the level of (high) court independence, following literature suggesting that independent courts contribute to building resilient democracies, as they play a positive role in policing the democratic compromise.[11] In fact, such findings are in line with the *telos* at the core of the design of independent judiciaries in modern constitutionalism that points directly towards the avoidance of tyranny.[12]
b. I also analyse the level of judicial corruption in each country, as more corrupt courts can be compromised and thus less able to constraint political actors. This is the case, for instance, as corruption can be a way through which political actors can control courts, thus preventing them from playing their expected role in policing the democratic compromise which, in turn, can disincentivize political actors from abiding by the rules of the democratic game.
c. Finally, I take into account the existence of a judicial council that is *de jure* independent from political actors[13] in a given country, as this arrangement has often been seen as a good practice of judicial governance that can protect democratic quality. Judicial councils that are independent from political actors are expected to protect judiciaries from political control and guarantee judicial independence.

Given the way these three conditions are measured (see the methods section in this chapter), the first two of them are closer to a *de facto* understanding of judicial independence and corruption, while for judicial councils I seek a *de jure* measurement. This is valuable, as the QCA models in this chapter will allow for analysis of how these different types of explanatory conditions interact in specific cases.

---

[10] Larkins (1996), p. 626.

[11] Staton, Reenock and Holsinger (2022), p. 141.

[12] Hamilton et al. (2003[1788]).

[13] For the operationalization of the category of judicial councils as 'independent' from political actors, see Chap. 2 and Appendix A.

Hypotheses

With this background, this chapter tests two hypotheses about the relationship between the above-mentioned factors and judicial governance. Since the focus of the analyses is on the model of independent judicial councils, my hypotheses are focused on this condition.

A first hypothesis (H1) posits that *the model of independent judicial councils is part of at least one configuration of conditions that is logically sufficient to the outcome 'high democratic quality'*. This is in line with the expectations about the positive role of this institution that has become a 'soft' standard in Europe. Note that the hypothesis does not suggest that this institution should be, alone, logically sufficient to achieve high levels of democratic quality. On the contrary, the expectation is one focused on logical complexity: independent judicial councils, in this hypothesis, are part of a larger logical configuration that includes other factors presented in this chapter.

The second hypothesis (H2) is the reverse of the first. It posits that *the absence of an independent judicial council is necessary to the outcome 'low democratic quality'*. This is for reasons similar to those behind the first hypothesis: if this institution is conducive to better levels of democratic quality, in countries with low democratic quality, we should find the absence of this model of judicial governance.

4.3 Methods

In this chapter, I take a different approach to understand the relationship between judicial governance and democratic quality, one in which the relationship between the conditions and the outcome is understood in terms of logical necessity and sufficiency. The analyses in this chapter are based on set theory, in which phenomena are operationalized as belonging or not to different sets. To do so, I used Qualitative Comparative Analysis (QCA).[14] In particular, I use the 'fuzzy set' variant of QCA, which allows cases to have gradations of their set membership.[15] This is because many of the conditions used were not dichotomous in nature, but rather membership of them was a matter of degree. Table 4.1 shows how the different explanatory conditions are operationalized ('calibrated') for these set-theoretical analyses.

As can be seen, the outcome selected for the analyses was the V-Dem Electoral Democracy Index. As explained earlier, this index measures 'the core value of making rulers responsive to citizens, achieved through electoral competition for the electorate's approval under circumstances when suffrage is extensive; political and civil society organizations can operate freely; elections are clean and not marred by fraud or systematic irregularities; and elections affect the composition of the chief

---

[14] Although some basic notions on how to interpret these analyses are presented in this book, readers willing to learn more about them can check the different existing works on the matter, including Adrian Dusa (2018); Rihoux and Ragin (2009); Schneider and Wagemann (2013).

[15] Schneider and Wagemann (2013), p. 13.

Table 4.1 Calibration of conditions for set-theoretical analyses

Condition label	Condition explanation	Source	Calibration
Edi	V-Dem Electoral Democracy Index (Outcome)	V-Dem[16]	High: > 0.65 Medium: 0.4–0.649 Low: < 0.4
GDP	GDP pc 2020	World Bank, Our world in data[17]	Full inclusion: 50,000 Cross-over: 30,000 Full exclusion: 10,000
Eu	Member States of the EU27 (post-Brexit)		1: Member State 0: Not a Member State
Nocorrupt	Absence of judicial corruption: WJP question 2.2	World Justice Project[18]	Full inclusion: 0.8 Cross-over point: 0.51 Full exclusion: 0.3
Indejudi	Independent judicial council	See Appendix	1: Independent Judicial councils 0: Any other
Hcourtindep	V-Dem High Court Independence Index	V-Dem[19]	Full inclusion: 3 Cross-over: −0.1 Full exclusion: −3

executive of the country. In between elections, there is freedom of expression and an independent media capable of presenting alternative views on matters of political relevance'.[20] Thus, this index does not include elements related to the rule of law or judicial institutions, and includes a rather minimalistic definition of democracy: one that is focused on the holding of regular, free, and fair elections. Such a definition of electoral democracy seems very close to the one recently used by Przeworski, and which the author conceptualizes as 'a political arrangement in which people select governments through elections and have a reasonable possibility of removing the incumbent governments they do not like'.[21]

From a research design perspective, the Electoral Democracy Index has an important advantage, as it minimizes the problem of endogeneity that could result from using as an outcome an index that included the role of courts in a democracy. From a theoretical perspective, using the Electoral Democracy Index also has advantages. In their recent book on abusive constitutional borrowing, Dixon and Landau also use a minimalistic definition of democracy 'centered around the idea that democracy entails a commitment to regular, free and fair elections, conducted on the basis

---

[16] Coppedge et al. (2021) V-Dem Codebook v.11.1.
[17] World Bank, Our World in Data (2020) GDP per capita (2020).
[18] (2021) World Justice Project—Rule of Law Index.
[19] Coppedge et al. (2021) V-Dem Codebook v.11.1.
[20] Ibid., p. 44.
[21] Przeworski (2019), p. 5.

4.3 Methods

of universal adult suffrage and competition between two and more parties'.[22] They argue that the main advantage of using such a definition for research purposes is its relative consensus: 'it is an idea of democracy that almost all political theorists can endorse, regardless of their particular, potentially more expansive understanding of democracy.[23] It is also a definition of democracy that draws on shared understandings of democracy at the transnational level—such as those incorporated in the Copenhagen criteria for accession to the European Union—and one that can be found in the majority of constitutional democracies around the world'.[24] It is worth emphasizing, though, that the use of this definition of democracy in this chapter is not the result of a normative adhesion to a minimalist concept of democracy in general. As stated above, the use of such minimalistic or thin definition of democracy to operationalize my outcome is the result of its adequacy at the theoretical and research design level for this particular piece of work.

QCA analyses will find out whether the relationship between an explanatory condition—or a combination of them—and an outcome is one of logical necessity, sufficiency, or neither. By logical necessity and sufficiency I simply mean what follows. A condition is logically necessary for an outcome when it is always present when the outcome occurs, although its presence does not guarantee occurrence.[25] A condition (or combination of conditions) is sufficient for an outcome when such an outcome is present every time the condition is observed, even if the outcome can also be present in instances in which the condition is not observed.[26]

The Electoral Democracy Index ranges from 0 to 1. However, when looking at the distribution of cases, three qualitatively different groups emerges: a group with high electoral democracy scores (above 0.65), a group with very low electoral democracy scores (below 0.4), and a group with intermediate scores. To account for this, three crisp outcomes were created.

The explanatory conditions were selected so that the models could shed some light on the relationship between wider political and socio-economic factors and factors related to judicial design. These included crisp and fuzzy conditions. GDP per capita was calibrated as a fuzzy condition with a cross-over point of 30,000, in order to have a balanced distribution within the sample, with full membership at 50,000 and full non-membership at 10,000. In the condition, 'high court independence' cases range between −2.8 and 3.4; to acknowledge for this, the cross-over point was selected at −0.1, with full inclusion at 3 and full exclusion at −3. Finally, judicial corruption was measured in an index ranging from 0 (highest levels of corruption) to 1 (lowest levels of corruption); the cross-over point was set at 0.51 (to disambiguate Serbia, whose score was 0.5), with full inclusion set at 0.8 and full exclusion at 0.3. It is worth noting that the source used to account for judicial corruption had no information for Azerbaijan, Montenegro, Armenia, Iceland, and Switzerland, so

---

[22] Dixon and Landau (2021), p. 24.
[23] Ibid., p. 26.
[24] Ibid., pp. 26–27.
[25] Ragin (2009), p. 109.
[26] For more details, see Schneider and Wagemann (2013), p. 76.

these cases were coded as missing for the analyses.[27] The rest of the conditions were crisp: EU membership (with the UK coded as a non-Member State), and presence of an independent judicial council (following the information of the Appendix).

Finally, it is worth making clear at this point that this chapter does not aim to provide a comprehensive causal model to explain the research outcome: the quality of electoral democracy. Instead, the aim of this chapter is much more modest: simply to test some conjectures which involve the role of judicial governance. More precisely, my aim is simply to falsify my configurational hypotheses in the context of my models, that is, I want to check whether there is evidence to reject my hypotheses. As it is always the case in the social sciences, the evidence provided in this chapter is not final. The ideas of 'necessity' and 'sufficiency' that connect the conditions to the outcome are understood simply in a logical sense and in the context of the models, in line with the explanation of these concepts provided earlier, so I avoid strong causal statements. Finally, in order to understand the phenomena explored, more evidence will be necessary in future research.

4.4 Analysis of Necessary Conditions

The analysis of necessary conditions explains which conditions are always present (or absent) when the outcome of interest occurs, even if the condition might also occur without the outcome occurring. Literature in the field suggests that for a condition to be considered as logically necessary for an outcome it must have a consistency of at least 0.9.[28]

Table 4.2 shows the analysis of necessary conditions for the different values of the outcome—high, intermediate, and low electoral democracy quality. As can be seen, for low quality of electoral democracy, there are two conditions that are technically necessary. One of them is the absence of independent judicial councils, meaning that all instances of low quality of electoral democracy were in countries without an independent judicial council. Examples of countries with low quality of electoral democracy in the sample include Azerbaijan, Russia, and Kazakhstan, all with hybrid or *sui generis* models. It also includes Belarus, in which the executive remains in control of judicial governance; and Turkey, which has a judicial council classified as not politically independent. The same occurs with EU membership: all of these instances of low quality of electoral democracy are also instances of countries outside the EU. Note, however, that both necessary conditions have a low coverage, which makes the relationship less meaningful.

For high quality of electoral democracy, the data is also interesting, especially with regards to two conditions: high level of high court independence (consistency

---

[27] As can be seen in the Appendix, in the QCA data matrix the relevant cells are simply empty for missing values on judicial corruption. fsQCA provides exactly the same solutions if the cases with missing values are removed from the analysis.

[28] Ibid., p. 143.

4.4 Analysis of Necessary Conditions

Table 4.2 Analyses of necessary conditions

	High electoral democracy quality		Intermediate electoral democracy quality		Low electoral democracy quality	
	Consistency	Coverage	Consistency	Coverage	Consistency	Coverage
IndepJcouncil	0.35	0.53	0.8	0.47	0	0
~Indepjcouncil	0.65	0.71	0.2	0.08	1	0.21
EUMS	0.92	0.89	0.3	0.11	0	0
~EUMS	0.08	0.14	0.7	0.5	1	0.36
GDP	0.78	0.86	0.19	0.08	0.29	0.06
~GDP	0.22	0.33	0.81	0.46	0.71	0.2
Highcourtindep	0.88	0.75	0.64	0.21	0.27	0.04
~Highcourtindep	0.12	0.31	0.36	0.34	0.72	0.35
Nocorrupt	0.96	0.74	0.54	0.16	0.65	0.1
~Nocorrupt	0.04	0.13	0.45	0.62	0.35	0.24

0.88) and absence of judicial corruption (consistency 0.96). High court independence cannot be technically considered as a necessary condition, but I believe that its consistency score is so close to the 0.9 threshold that it makes it equally substantively meaningful. The interpretation of these results points to these two conditions being present every time that a country has a high level of electoral democracy quality. This is relevant also in relation to the independent judicial council model, which is far from the 0.9 consistency threshold for this outcome. This suggests that while an independent, non-corrupt judiciary is necessary for the outcome 'high quality of electoral democracy', such an independent and non-corrupt judiciary does not need to be achieved through the implementation of the model of independent judicial councils. A good example of this is Spain. This country has a judicial council that has not been classified as politically independent: as previously explained, the members of the Spanish judicial council (CGPJ) are appointed by the Parliament, although following consensual cross-party procedures. This parliamentary role in the appointments was compatible with high levels of high court independence, low levels of judicial corruption, and a high quality of electoral democracy.

Finally, it is worth mentioning that GDP does not reach the 0.9 threshold for any of the outcomes, despite the strong correlation with democratic quality that this variable exhibited in Chap. 3. This suggests that, even if economic development is positively correlated to democratic quality, high levels of electoral democracy quality occurred in some instances even in the absence of high levels of GDP. The analysis also suggests that a low GDP is not logically necessary in order to exhibit a low quality of electoral democracy.

4.5 Analyses of Sufficient Conditions

The analysis of sufficiency shows which conditions—or combinations of them—are sufficient for the outcome to occur, meaning that every time that the condition—or combination of conditions—occur, the outcome also can be observed. Table 4.3 presents the analysis of sufficient conditions for the presence of high electoral democracy quality. The model has a moderate coverage level (0.683) but a very high consistency (0.929). This means that what the paths in the model cover is to a very large extent the outcome of interest, even if the phenomena explored—high quality of electoral democracy—is not fully explained by the model.

The model consists of a combination of high GDP, EU membership, lack of judicial corruption, and high court independence. These four conditions, combined, are logically sufficient to the presence of the outcome. They point at a combination of economic-political background conditions (GDP and EU membership) together with a solid institutional judicial architecture. Note, however, that in this path there is a condition missing: the condition referred to independent judicial councils is irrelevant to this path. This means that the presence or absence of this model of judicial governance is logically irrelevant for the achievement of the outcome. That is not to say that judicial conditions are not part of the logically sufficient path to a high quality of electoral democracy: as already noted, together with high GDP

Table 4.3 Analysis of sufficient conditions for the presence of high electoral democracy quality

Path	Raw coverage	Unique coverage	Consistency	Cases
Gdp*EU* Nocorrupt* Highcourtindep	0.683	0.683	0.929	Denmark (0.95,1), Sweden (0.94,1), Austria (0.93,1), Ireland (0.92,1), Finland (0.91,1), Germany (0.87,1), Netherlands (0.87,1), Belgium (0.86,1), Luxembourg (0.85,1), France (0.84,1), Malta (0.8,1), Italy (0.79,1), Czechia (0.78,1), Cyprus (0.76,1), Lithuania (0.73,1), Slovenia (0.73,1), Spain (0.72,1), Estonia (0.7,1), Poland (0.58,0), Portugal (0.58,1)

Solution coverage: 0.683
Solution consistency: 0.929

Consistency cut-off: 0.9. Directional expectations: all conditions are expected to contribute to the outcome when present

4.5 Analyses of Sufficient Conditions

Table 4.4 Analysis of sufficient conditions for intermediate electoral democracy quality

Path	Raw coverage	Unique coverage	Consistency	Cases
~GDP* ~EU* Highcourtindep* Indepjcouncil	0.453	0.453	1	Moldova (0.8,1), BiH (0.75,1), Kosovo (0.72,1), Georgia (0.7,1), Albania (0.61,1), Ukraine (0.53,1)

Solution coverage: 0.453
Solution consistency: 1

Consistency cut-off: 0.9. Directional expectations: all conditions are expected to contribute to the outcome when present or absent

and EU membership, the path requires the presence of an independent, non-corrupt judiciary. But the model shows that this type of judiciary can be achieved both with an independent judicial council (as in Italy and France) or without it (for instance, in Denmark or Czechia). Interestingly, this finding seems to be in line with literature in the field that also suggests that high levels of judicial empowerment can be achieved in the absence of the judicial council model.[29]

The analysis for intermediate levels of democratic quality is presented in Table 4.4. The model has a more modest coverage (0.453) but a perfect consistency (1) score. It shows one logically sufficient path to intermediate levels of electoral democracy quality.

The path shows a combination of absence of the political (EU membership) and economic (GDP) background conditions together with the presence of a solid judicial-institutional architecture. The latter consists of a combination of high court independence and judicial councils which are, at least *de jure*, politically independent. The model of an independent judicial council, which was logically irrelevant to high quality of electoral democracy, is not—in this model—logically irrelevant to moderate levels of the outcome. Note that there is an additional difference between this path and the model to high quality of electoral democracy: the background conditions GDP and EU membership, which were present for the logically sufficient path to high democratic quality (Table 4.3), are, as already indicated, absent in this model (Table 4.4).

Table 4.5 presents the analysis of sufficient conditions for cases with a low quality of electoral democracy. Again, the model presents a moderate coverage (0.71) and a relatively high consistency (0.96). The model, however, presents a very interesting path, consisting in the combined absence of high GDP, of EU membership, and of an independent judicial council. The model, thus, shows that the absence of independent judicial councils is part of the logically sufficient configurations for the outcome. This is consistent with the findings of the analysis of necessary conditions.

A comparative look at Tables 4.4 and 4.5 reveals again some interesting patterns that can be illustrated with reference to specific cases. Both the cases covered by Table 4.4 and Table 4.5 are cases with lower levels of GDP and absence of EU

---

[29] Šipulová et al. (2022).

Table 4.5 Analysis of sufficient conditions for low electoral democracy quality

Path	Raw coverage	Unique coverage	Consistency	Cases
~GDP* ~EU* ~Indepjcouncil	0.71	0.71	0.96	Serbia (0.85,1), Belarus (0.84,1), Kazakhstan (0.67,1), Russia (0.63,1), Turkey (0.56,1)

Solution coverage: 0.71
Solution consistency: 0.96

Consistency cut-off: 0.85. Directional expectations: all conditions are expected to contribute to the outcome when absent

membership. But what differentiates them was the institutional architecture of the judicial branch. While countries such as Moldova have good levels of high court independence and an independent judicial council, countries including Russia and Turkey are marked by the lack of such independent judicial council. These latter countries exhibit very poor levels of quality of electoral democracy, while countries with a good institutional architecture of the judicial branch display at least moderate levels of such outcome.

4.6 Conclusion

This chapter has shed some new light on the relationship between judicial governance and democracy, although this time from a configurational, case-oriented perspective. The findings, from the perspective of judicial governance, point at two main takeaways.

First, the model of independent judicial councils seems to be logically irrelevant for cases of high electoral democracy quality, and thus, my hypothesis 1 did not find support. But this model of judicial governance was not logically irrelevant, in the context of the models, for intermediate levels (for which it was present) or low levels of the outcome (for which it was absent). Additionally, the absence of independent judicial councils was logically necessary for the presence of low quality of electoral democracy, thus supporting empirically hypothesis 2, even if the coverage of the necessary condition was low. The evidence, thus, does not allow us to discard the suggestion that this model of judicial governance might have after all a certain relationship to democratic quality, even if such relationship could be more nuanced than what a statistical correlation would involve, and even if its relevance is limited to some subsets of the cases. The judicial council model has been found to have negative effects on a number of fronts. For instance, it has been suggested that it can lead to reduced judicial accountability and increased corporatism.[30] My findings do not refute that strand of literature, as they focus on a different object of study. But such findings do add complexity to the picture, by showing an interesting aspect of the relationship between independent judicial councils and democratic quality.

---

[30] Spáč, Šipulová, and Urbániková (2018).

Second, the models point at other conditions related to the justice system as logically relevant to the outcome. Take the example of the level of high court independence or absence of judicial corruption. These conditions often featur in a prominent place in the models of logical sufficiency. For high levels of electoral democracy quality, in particular, a high level of high court independence and a low level of judicial corruption was a part of the configuration, while the existence or not of an independent judicial council was irrelevant. This finding is also backed to a large extent by the analysis of necessary conditions.

Finally, on a methodological note, this chapter has shown the usefulness of complementing statistical analyses with configurational ones. Each type of method can shed light on different aspects of the phenomena explored and, in this case, their complementary use allows for a very interesting understanding of the connection between judicial governance and democracy.

References

M Coppedge J Gerring CH Knutsen et al (2021) V-Dem Codebook v.11.1

R Dixon D Landau 2021 Abusive constitutional borrowing Oxford University Press USA

Dusa A (2018) QCA with R. A comprehensive resource. Springer International Publishing. Springer, New York

B Epperly 2019 The political foundations of judicial independence in dictatorship and democracy Oxford University Press Great Britain

DM Gibler KA Randazzo 2011 Testing the effects of independent judiciaries on the likelihood of democratic backsliding Am J Polit Sci 55 696 709 https://doi.org/10.1111/j.1540-5907.2010.00504.x

PA Hall RCR Taylor 1996 Political science and the three new institutionalisms Polit Stud 44 936 957 https://doi.org/10.1111/j.1467-9248.1996.tb00343.x

Hamilton A, Madison J, Jay J (2003[1788]) The federalist: with letters of Brutus. Cambridge University Press, Cambridge

R Inglehart 2018 Cultural evolution Cambridge University Press UK

MG Laebens A Lührmann 2021 What halts democratic erosion? The changing role of accountability Democratization 28 908 928 https://doi.org/10.1080/13510347.2021.1897109

CM Larkins 1996 Judicial independence and democratization: a theoretical and conceptual analysis Am J Comp Law 44 605 626 https://doi.org/10.2307/840623

SM Lipset 1959 Some social requisites of democracy: economic development and political legitimacy Am Polit Sci Rev 53 69 105 https://doi.org/10.2307/1951731

L Pech KL Scheppele 2017 Illiberalism within: rule of law backsliding in the EU Camb Yearb Eur Leg Stud 19 3 47 https://doi.org/10.1017/cel.2017.9

Popova M (2012) Politicized justice in emerging democracies : a study of courts in Russia and Ukraine/[electronic resource]. Cambridge : Cambridge University Press, 2012, Cambridge

A Przeworski 2019 Crises of democracy Cambridge University Press UK

Ragin C (2009) Qualitative comparative analysis using fuzzy sets (fsQCA). In: Rihoux B, Ragin C (eds) Configurational comparative methods. Qualitative Comparative Analysis (QCA) and Related Techniques. Sage, USA, pp 87–122

KA Randazzo DM Gibier R Reid 2016 Examining the development of judicial independence Polit Res Q 69 583 593

Rihoux B, Ragin CC (eds) (2009) Configurational comparative methods. Qualitative Comparative Analysis (QCA) and Related Techniques. Sage, US

F Schimmelfennig H Scholtz 2008 EU democracy promotion in the European neighbourhood: political conditionality, economic development and transnational exchange Eur Union Polit 9 187 215 https://doi.org/10.1177/1465116508089085

CQ Schneider C Wagemann 2013 Set-theoretic methods for the social sciences Cambridge University Press, UK A Guide to Qualitative Comparative Analysis

Šipulová k, Spáč S, Kosař D, Papoušková T, Derka V (2022) Judicial Self-Governance Index: towards better understanding of the role of judges in governing the judiciary. Regul Gov. https://doi.org/10.1111/rego.12453

S Spáč K Šipulová M Urbániková 2018 Capturing the judiciary from inside: the story of judicial self-governance in Slovakia Ger Law J 19 7 1741 1768 https://doi.org/10.1017/S2071832200023221

JK Staton C Reenock J Holsinger 2022 Can courts be bulwarks of democracy? Cambridge University Press, Cambridge Judges and the Politics of Prudence

Open Access This chapter is licensed under the terms of the Creative Commons Attribution 4.0 International License (http://creativecommons.org/licenses/by/4.0/), which permits use, sharing, adaptation, distribution and reproduction in any medium or format, as long as you give appropriate credit to the original author(s) and the source, provide a link to the Creative Commons license and indicate if changes were made.

The images or other third party material in this chapter are included in the chapter's Creative Commons license, unless indicated otherwise in a credit line to the material. If material is not included in the chapter's Creative Commons license and your intended use is not permitted by statutory regulation or exceeds the permitted use, you will need to obtain permission directly from the copyright holder.

Chapter 5
Conclusions and Some Policy Reflections

5.1 The Complex Relationship Between Judicial Governance and Democracy: Summary of Findings of This Research

In this book, I have analysed the relationship between models of judicial governance and democracy. To do so, I have relied on a newly gathered database of all models of judicial governance in all European countries—except for the smallest countries—which is to the best of this author's knowledge the first comprehensive database of these organs in the region (see Table 1.1 and Appendix A).

My findings point at the relationship between judicial governance and democratic quality being rather complex so that explaining such relationship will require some nuances. At first sight, European countries relying on a judicial council have on average democracies of worse quality than countries relying on models such as the courts service. This was the case even for those judicial councils whose design provided, at least formally, some insulation from political actors. This is striking, as the judicial council model has become the standard recommendation by European institutions and international best practice when it comes to managing the judiciary.

However, such a negative correlation between democratic quality and the presence of a judicial council seemed to be hiding the impact of other factors. Judicial councils were often implemented in Europe in countries in transition from authoritarian regimes to democracies. According to modernization theory,[1] democratization is strongly linked to economic development. Nevertheless, countries do not have equal levels of economic development, which could translate into different levels of democratization. With this background, this research hypothesized that at equal levels of economic development, having a judicial council might not be negatively correlated to democratic quality after all. My results in Chap. 3 pointed in that direction.

---
[1] See Inglehart (2018); Lipset (1959).

In fact, as suggested by my configurational models in Chap. 4, judicial councils that were at least *de jure* independent from political actors were not always logically relevant to democratic quality. Many countries had high levels of electoral democracy quality regardless of their model of judicial governance. But conversely, countries with low levels of democratic quality never had an independent judicial council, and the absence of this institution was part of the logically sufficient path to such outcome. The impact of judicial governance on democratic quality, thus, cannot be discarded, even if this might be occurring in forms that are frequently counterintuitive and in different ways for different types of countries.

In this chapter, I take stock of the findings of this book. In the next section, I do this at the policy level, presenting some evidence-based reflections to be taken into account when designing models of judicial governance. In the following section, I discuss the main limitations of this research and the challenges that lie ahead for research about judicial governance. Next, I warn against the idea that only democratic quality matters when assessing the adequacy of models of judicial governance. The final part concludes the chapter and the book.

5.2 Some Evidence-Based Policy Reflections

So far there has been a significant amount of academic and political discussion about judicial governance and democracy. However, unfortunately, little evidence has been provided at the empirical level about the relationship between these two questions. The aim of this book was to contribute to filling this important gap. Evidence-based approaches can help policymakers improve models of judicial governance. In particular, empirical evidence can help design judicial governance in such a way that it provides for better quality democracies, at a time at which democratic systems of government seem to be under stress in several countries. Based on the findings of this research, some reflections can be put forward. These reflections should however be taken with a grain of salt: they are based on the provisional evidence gathered in this research. Such evidence is, I believe, robust, even if I have tried to phrase it and present it in the most cautious possible way. But as it is the case in general in the social sciences, my findings will need further research and confirmation (see more on this in the last part of this chapter).

5.2.1 Ensuring Independent, Non-corrupt Judiciaries

In my QCA analyses, the independence of the court system seems to be particularly important when understanding the quality of electoral democracy of the countries.

5.2 Some Evidence-Based Policy Reflections 63

Countries with a high quality of electoral democracy were very frequently countries in which (high) courts were highly independent and levels of judicial corruption were low, even if these conditions alone were not logically sufficient to such outcome. Instead, they were combined with other conditions such as high GDP and EU membership.

If, as the models in this book seem to suggest, high court independence and absence of judicial corruption matter, then policy efforts around judicial governance have good reasons to focus on the achievement of these two values. This is so for two reasons. First, because judicial independence and absence of corruption are normatively valuable in themselves. Second, also, because if the analyses in this research point in the right direction, judicial independence and absence of corruption might be important ingredients of the recipe for solid democracies. Note, however, that countries with high levels of high court independence and low levels of corruption were not always countries following the model of independent judicial councils. And also note that such model of judicial governance was logically irrelevant to the outcome 'high quality of electoral democracy'. All this points to one interesting conclusion: the struggle for independent and non-corrupt judiciaries is very strongly connected to, but is not the same thing as, the push for the dissemination of the judicial council model. I elaborate more on this below.

5.2.2 The Judicial Council Model is not a Bad Arrangement after all ...

Earlier in this book I discussed different mechanisms of judicial governance, as well as their theoretical advantages and disadvantages. My analyses in Chap. 3 presented evidence against the idea that they could be negatively associated to the quality of democracy. The analyses in Chap. 4 showed that, albeit the model of independent judicial councils is irrelevant to explain high levels of electoral democracy quality, its absence is a logically necessary condition for low levels of electoral democracy quality, and part of the sufficient path to such outcome.

The model of independent judicial councils is thus, after all, not a bad arrangement. Countries with low levels of electoral democracy quality had all in common the absence of this approach to judicial governance. With similar background conditions (lower levels of GDP and lack of EU membership), countries with an independent judicial council (and low levels of judicial corruption) displayed better levels of democratic quality than countries without it. And the logical irrelevance of the model of independent judicial councils for high quality of electoral democracy does not mean that this arrangement is detrimental to democratic quality, but simply that such outcome occurred in the sample with or without it.

5.2.3 ... but Alternatives to the Judicial Council Model Should not be Discarded

The judicial council model is thus not a bad arrangement. But what happens with the other approaches to judicial governance?

Many countries will not be willing to implement the model of strong and independent councils at all. And this might not be a problem. As explained, the model of independent judicial councils appears in my analysis to be irrelevant to high levels of quality of electoral democracy. Put differently, countries can achieve exemplary electoral democracies without this approach to judicial governance. In fact, this finding is in line with the most recent literature in the field regarding the relationship between judicial governance and judicial independence. In their work, Šipulova et al. showed evidence that judicial empowerment is possible in the absence of the existence of the judicial council model, and even under the Ministry of Justice model.[2]

For that reason, in some cases, the existence of other models of judicial governance might be a legitimate choice. Put in other terms, for countries that have a functional model of judicial governance different from that of strong and independent councils, preserving it might be a good idea. This could be the case, for instance, if that model of judicial governance performs well with regards to the maximization of values such as judicial independence, accountability, efficacy, or democracy protection.

The idea that countries can opt for alternatives to the model of independent judicial council is, however, subject to some conditions. This model was not part of the sufficient path for high electoral democracy quality. But other conditions were a combination of high GDP, membership of the EU, and independent, non-corrupt judiciaries. Absent these or other conditions that might lead to high quality of electoral democracy, countries should be cautious in dispensing with the model of independent judicial councils, given that the absence of this institution was a necessary condition for a low quality of electoral democracy.

Furthermore, models of judicial governance that undermine aspects such as judicial independence or that allow judicial corruption can be, for that reason, a risk to democratic quality. Countries with high levels of electoral democracy quality should thus be cautious too, and ought to avoid the implementation of such models of judicial governance if they want to remain high-quality democracies.

---

[2] Šipulova et al. (2022:1).

5.3 'Then, are We Sure that We Understand the Relation Between Judicial Governance and Democracy'. Limitations of this Research and Future Research Challenges

As I advanced in Chap. 1, when preparing this book I had three aims in mind. My first aim was to make an academic contribution to the understanding of the complex, paradoxical, and often counterintuitive relationship between judicial governance and democracy. My second aim was to put forward some policy reflections, contributing to the debate about how to achieve better and more resilient models of judicial governance. Last but not least, I wanted to contribute to the public debate about judicial governance, providing explanations that are as clear as possible on this subject.

In reading this book, social scientists will understand that the empirical findings are, like all findings in our disciplines, subject to shortcomings and limitations. But since I want to make a contribution to public debate about judicial governance, the general readership of this book deserves some transparency in these regards. In particular, contributing to the public debate with this book involves acknowledging that my analyses should also be subject to criticism and scrutiny. In particular, I suggest my readers pay attention to a number of aspects.

First, classifying countries into models of judicial governance is a difficult task. As I said earlier in this book, any classification is apt for contestation, perhaps even controversy. And this is not only because definitions—such as those of judicial councils, courts services, or Ministry of Justice models—have always an inherent degree of vagueness that we can minimize but not eradicate. It is also because the sources of information are always limited, and because cases are frequently so *sui generis* that they are difficult to classify. As my analysis is built upon those difficult and contestable classifications, they should always be taken cautiously.

A second aspect that I wanted to remark on is that my analysis captures a static picture of the relationship between judicial governance and democracy. I focused on organs of judicial governance and indicators of democratic quality as they were at the time of writing this book. A longitudinal study—that is to say, one which takes into account the time dimension and the historical evolution of the object of study—would be a better alternative. However, unavoidable limitations in the research—including, but not limited to, the availability of information and resources—suggest this would be a fruitful avenue to explore in the future. Still, it is necessary to admit that including the historical dimension in the analyses would be much more informative and make the findings much more robust.

Something similar happened with the geographic scope of this book. The analysis of this research, restricted to European countries, was interesting for several reasons. First, the variation within the sample of countries with regards to types of approaches to judicial governance and democratic quality allowed me to carry out meaningful analysis. Additionally, regional specific factors, such as the Europeanizing pressures in favour of the implementation of the judicial council model, rendered the countries in my sample particularly suitable for this type of exploration. However, for obvious reasons, analyses covering other world regions—perhaps the whole of the globe—would be a fantastic development to the research undertaken in this book.

The research choices made also matter. For instance, to account for whether an organ for judicial governance was *de jure* 'politically independent' I focused on the organ appointing its members. I believe that this was the right choice: after all, literature on Judicial Politics has discussed the phenomenon of 'loyalty to the appointer' in judicial-type institutions,[3] so there were reasons to think that such phenomenon takes place also in organs for judicial governance. However, this was not the only operationalization option available: a different operationalization could have focused, for instance, on the professional background of members of the organs, rather than on their appointers.

Finally, there are inherent limitations to some of my specific analysis. These often had to do with the small size of my sample: with only 46 cases, I opted for a conservative approach to many of these analyses, trying to minimize the number of variables used—that is to say, trying to explore only a small number of explanations at the same time. Fortunately, the use of QCA as a complement to statistics allowed me to include more factors and explanations in my models, thus accounting for the complexity of the object of this study.

5.3.1 *Judicial Governance Beyond Democratic Quality*

One final warning about this book has to do with its focus: the relationship between judicial governance and democratic quality. Democratic quality is extremely important, and it should be taken into account when designing models of judicial governance. But democratic quality, important as it is, is not the only thing that matters. Judicial governance might have implications for many other important aspects of democratic societies. Does the model for judicial governance of a certain country contribute to achieving an efficient judiciary? What about an independent judiciary? And what about the fight against judicial corruption?

I will provide an example of why these questions are important. We can think about Spain, where an ongoing controversy exists on the question of who should appoint the members of the Judicial Council.[4] If the findings of this book are correct, it might be thought that democratic quality is not a strong argument in favour or against the current system of appointment, where the parliament appoints the members of the *Consejo General del Poder Judicial* by a super-majority. This is because for high-quality democracies (like Spain) the model of judicial governance seemed to be scarcely relevant, as it disappeared from the solution for the sufficiency of that outcome. This would be also the case because the statistical analyses were not able to

---

[3] For instance, Garoupa et al. (2021).
[4] Castillo-Ortiz (2022); Hernández González (2022); Pérez (2018).

find a significant correlation between models of judicial governance and democratic quality in terms of net effects.

However, that idea (the irrelevance of the debate on judicial governance for a country like Spain) should be dismissed quickly. First, because the book actually shows that judicial governance does seem to matter in certain ways for democratic quality: for instance, the absence of independent judicial councils seemed to be a logically necessary condition for authoritarian rule. Furthermore, as said above, a model of judicial governance which undermined aspects such as judicial independence and increased judicial corruption could be a direct risk for democratic quality, as these factors do feature in my analysis as relevant in cases of high quality of electoral democracy. Given that countries can suffer from democratic erosion, even high-quality democracies should thus be wary of the idea that judicial governance is irrelevant for them.

The second reason is connected to the former. The debate about judicial governance (in Spain as in any other country) should not be only about how organs for the governance of the judicial branch directly contribute to democratic quality, even if that topic should always be a priority one. The debate should be also, as I said before, about other aspects, such as the contribution of the design of judicial governance to the fight for judicial independence, the rule of law, judicial efficiency, and against corruption. These aspects will often be related to democratic quality, but they also matter in themselves. Unfortunately, we still have very little empirical evidence on these important aspects.

5.4 Judicial Governance Matters

The politics of judicial governance are here to stay. Policymakers will always have to opt for competing designs of judicial governance. In so doing, they will have to evaluate how each model of judicial governance performs vis-à-vis the maximization of certain values. Democratic leaders will want to maximize judicial independence, accountability, and the capacity of the judiciary to protect democracy. Authoritarian leaders will prefer models of judicial governance that maximize judicial submission to the executive. Unfortunately, we have seen the latter approach in many of the countries explored in this book.

So far, we know very little about how each model of judicial governance actually performs in relation to their declared institutional goals. Organs for judicial governance should be assessed against a large number of standards, and in a number of different dimensions: from their capacity to efficiently manage resources to their ability to increase judicial independence or accountability. Their contribution to democratic quality is only one of the institutional goals against which the performance of organs of judicial governance should be measured. But it is a very important one. At the end of the day, the question of judicial governance is present in many accounts of processes of rule of law backsliding.[5]

However, so far the evidence in this area had been scarce. We simply did not know very well which designs of organs of judicial governance have a better capacity to contribute to the quality of democracy in different countries, and why. With this book, I hope to have contributed to our understanding of this very important issue.

References

Castillo-Ortiz P (2022) El gobierno de la judicatura en España. In: Informe sobre la Democracia en España 2021. Fundación Alternativas, pp 33–44
Garoupa N, Gili M, Gómez Pomar F (2021) Loyalty to the party or loyalty to the party leader: evidence from the Spanish constitutional court. Int Rev Law Econ 67:105999. https://doi.org/10.1016/j.irle.2021.105999
Hernández González G (2022) La independencia de Consejo General del Poder Judicial en España: una perspectiva comparada con los países del entorno y propuestas de mejora. Fund Altern
Inglehart R (2018) Cultural evolution. Cambridge University Press, UK
Lipset SM (1959) Some social requisites of democracy: economic development and political legitimacy. Am Polit Sci Rev 53:69–105. https://doi.org/10.2307/1951731
Pérez AT (2018) Judicial self-government and judicial independence: the political capture of the general council of the judiciary in Spain. Ger Law J 19:1769–1800. https://doi.org/10.1017/S2071832200023233
Sadurski W (2019) Poland's constitutional breakdown. Oxford University Press
Šipulová K, Spáč S, Kosař D, Papoušková T, Derka V (2022) Judicial Self-Governance Index: towards better understanding of the role of judges in governing the judiciary. Regul Gov. https://doi.org/10.1111/rego.12453

Open Access This chapter is licensed under the terms of the Creative Commons Attribution 4.0 International License (http://creativecommons.org/licenses/by/4.0/), which permits use, sharing, adaptation, distribution and reproduction in any medium or format, as long as you give appropriate credit to the original author(s) and the source, provide a link to the Creative Commons license and indicate if changes were made.

The images or other third party material in this chapter are included in the chapter's Creative Commons license, unless indicated otherwise in a credit line to the material. If material is not included in the chapter's Creative Commons license and your intended use is not permitted by statutory regulation or exceeds the permitted use, you will need to obtain permission directly from the copyright holder.

---

[5] See, for instance, Sadurski (2019).

Appendix A
Classification and Justification of Models of Judicial Governance

Country	Model of Judicial Governance: justification	Independent organ for judicial governance (only possible when based on judicial council of courts service): justification (at least half of members must not be elected by political actors)	Sources
Albania	Judicial Council: High Judicial Council has powers over judicial careers, including proposing candidates to the Supreme Court, career development, and discipline of judges	Yes: 6 of 11 members elected by the General Meeting of Judges	Official website[1]
Andorra	Excluded from sample		
Armenia	Hybrid/Other: There is a Council of Justice, but its powers over careers are shared with the President of the Republic	No: the country is not based on judicial council or courts service models (for the Council of Justice, five members elected by the parliament and five members elected by peer judges)	Constitution

(continued)

---

[1] http://klgj.al/rreth-nesh/ (accessed 10.09.2022).

(continued)

Country	Model of Judicial Governance: justification	Independent organ for judicial governance (only possible when based on judicial council of courts service): justification (at least half of members must not be elected by political actors)	Sources
Austria	Ministry of Justice: see source	No: no autonomous organ for judicial governance exists	Specialized literature[2]
Azerbaijan	Hybrid/Other: the Act of the Judicial and Legal Council gives this organ powers over judicial careers. However, political actors retain significant powers over judicial appointments and careers	No: not based on judicial council of courts service (Art. 6.2 of Law on the Judicial and Legal Council determines membership of the council in their majority by either political actors or by judicial or legal professionals that are themselves politically appointed)	Constitution Official website, law on the Council[3] Helsinki Foundation for Human Rights Report[4]
Belarus	Ministry of Justice: the President (but not the Ministry of Justice) concentrates powers over judicial careers	No: no autonomous organ for judicial governance exists	UN Special Rapporteur on Human Rights in Belarus[5]
Belgium	Courts Service: borderline case, but the institution has limited, shared competences over judicial careers, with virtually no disciplinary competences	Yes: 22 members elected by peer judges and 22 members elected by political actors	ENCJ factsheet[6]

(continued)

---

[2] Bobek and Kosar (2014).
[3] http://www.judicialcouncil.gov.az/law/ar/emhs.pdf (accessed 10.09.2022).
[4] https://www.nhc.nl/assets/uploads/2017/07/Functioning-of-the-Judicial-System-in-Azerbaijan-and-its-Impact-on-the-Right-to-A-Fair-Trial.pdf (accessed 10.09.2022).
[5] https://www.refworld.org.es/topic,57f504720,57f50912c1,53a0272a4,0,,,BLR.html (accessed 10.09.2022).
[6] https://www.encj.eu/images/stories/pdf/factsheets/hrj_csj_belgium.pdf (accessed 10.09.2022).

Appendix A: Classification and Justification of Models of Judicial Governance 71

(continued)

Country	Model of Judicial Governance: justification	Independent organ for judicial governance (only possible when based on judicial council of courts service): justification (at least half of members must not be elected by political actors)	Sources
Bosnia and Herzegovina	Judicial Council: wide competences over judicial careers	Yes: most members not elected by political actors	Law on the council[7]
Bulgaria	Judicial Council: wide range of competences including appointment, assignment, transfer, and promotion of judges, as well as disciplinary competences	Yes: 11 members elected by judicial actors, 11 members elected by parliament, and 3 ex officio members from high courts	JS2016, Specialized literature,[8] ENCJ factsheet
Croatia	Judicial Council: wide competences over judicial careers, including appointment, reassignment, discipline, and dismissal of judges	Yes: 7 out of 11 members elected by peer judges	JS2016, OECD[9] ENCJ factsheet
Cyprus	Hybrid/Other: there is a Supreme Council of Judicature, but the President elects Supreme Court judges, which are a big proportion of the national judiciary and that compose the Supreme Council of Judicature	No: not based on judicial council or courts service models (Supreme Council of Judicature is composed by Supreme Court judges, that are elected by the President of the Republic)	Constitution, Official website[10]
Czechia	Ministry of Justice: see source	No: as no autonomous organ for judicial governance exists	Specialized literature[11]

(continued)

---

[7] https://www.venice.coe.int/webforms/documents/default.aspx?pdffile=CDL-REF(2021)007-E (accessed 10.09.2022).
[8] Castillo-Ortiz (2017).
[9] OECD (2019).
[10] http://www.supremecourt.gov.cy/judicial/sc.nsf/dmljudiciary_en/dmljudiciary_en?opendocument (accessed 10.09.2022).
[11] Bobek and Kosar (2014).

(continued)

Country	Model of Judicial Governance: justification	Independent organ for judicial governance (only possible when based on judicial council of courts service): justification (at least half of members must not be elected by political actors)	Sources
Denmark	Courts Service: no significant competences over judicial careers	Yes: members formally appointed by Minister, but on recommendation of legal and other institutions	JS2016,[12] official website[13]
Estonia	Judicial Council (weak): limited powers over careers	Yes: majority are elected by peer judges or by other legal associations or are lawyers that are ex officio members	Specialized literature,[14] Estonian Courts Act, official website[15]
Finland	Courts Service: National Courts Administration was recently created	No: managed by a Board of Administrators mostly coming from judicial positions, but whose members are appointed by the Government	Official website Rule of Law Report Finland[16]
France	Judicial Council: wide competences over judicial careers, including judicial nominations and discipline	Yes: for '*magistrats du siège*' there is no majority of members appointed by political actors	ENCJ factsheet
Georgia	Judicial Council: powers over judicial careers	Yes: majority of members elected by peer judges	Constitution
Germany	Ministry of Justice: see source	No: as no autonomous organ for judicial governance exists	Specialized literature[17]

(continued)

---

[12] Castillo-Ortiz (2017).
[13] https://domstol.dk/om-os/domstolsstyrelsen (accessed 10.09.2022).
[14] Castillo-Ortiz (2019).
[15] https://www.riigikohus.ee/en/administration-courts/council-administration-courts (accessed 10.09.2022).
[16] https://ec.europa.eu/info/sites/info/files/2020_rule_of_law_report_-_input_from_member_states_-_finland.pdf (accessed 10.09.2022).
[17] Bobek and Kosar (2014).

Appendix A: Classification and Justification of Models of Judicial Governance 73

(continued)

Country	Model of Judicial Governance: justification	Independent organ for judicial governance (only possible when based on judicial council of courts service): justification (at least half of members must not be elected by political actors)	Sources
Greece	Judicial Council (weak): see source	Yes: most members elected by lot	Specialized literature,[18] official website of Council of State[19]
Hungary	Hybrid/Other: Hungary has de facto two organs for judicial governance. The National Judicial Council with managerial powers, and the National Judicial Office with powers over judicial careers	No: not based on a judicial council or courts service model, but on a hybrid of the two (National Judicial Council is elected by judges, but more powerful National Judicial Office, and in particular its President, is politically appointed)	ENCJ factsheet, Specialized literature[20]
Iceland	Courts Service: functions are mostly about management of the judiciary	Yes: out of 5 members, 4 are elected by peer judges and appointed by the Minister of Justice	Dómstólasýslan
Ireland	Courts Service: no significant competences on judicial careers	Yes: most members elected by judges or law professionals	ENCJ factsheet, official website of Courts Service
Italy	Judicial Council: wide range of competences over judicial careers	Yes: only a minority elected by political actors, most members are elected by their peers	ENCJ factsheets, official website of Consiglio Superiore della Magistratura
Kazakhstan	Hybrid/Other: there is a High Judicial Council with powers over judicial careers, but they are exercised jointly with the executive	No: not based on judicial council or courts service models (members of High Judicial Council are appointed by the executive branch)	Constitution, Law on the High Judicial Council[21]

(continued)

---

[18] Castillo-Ortiz (2019).

[19] http://www.adjustice.gr/webcenter/portal/SteEn/Home?_afrLoop=23439127860043331#!%40%40%3F_afrLoop%3D23439127860043331%26centerWidth%3D100%2525%26showHeader%3Dtrue%26_adf.ctrl-state%3Dffos8lt5_4 (accessed 10.09.2022).

[20] Szente (2021).

[21] https://www.venice.coe.int/webforms/documents/default.aspx?pdffile=CDL-REF(2018)050-E (accessed 10.09.2022).

(continued)

Country	Model of Judicial Governance: justification	Independent organ for judicial governance (only possible when based on judicial council of courts service): justification (at least half of members must not be elected by political actors)	Sources
Kosovo	Judicial Council: the Constitution grants the judicial council powers over judicial careers	Yes: a majority of members are elected by peer judges	Constitution
Latvia	Courts Service: very limited competences on judicial careers	Yes: majority are members elected by peer judges or are judicial ex officio members	ENCJ factsheet
Liechtenstein	Excluded from sample		
Lithuania	Judicial Council: wide range of competences over judicial careers	Yes: majority of members elected by peer judges	ENCJ factsheet, official website
Luxembourg	Hybrid/Other: see source	No: not based on judicial council of courts service models	Specialized literature[22]
Malta	Courts Service: very limited competences on judicial careers	Yes, only a minority appointed by political actors	ENCJ factsheet
Moldova	Judicial Council: Constitution of Moldova gives the council powers over judicial careers	Yes: half of members elected by peer judges, and President of Supreme Court is ex officio member	Constitution, Specialized literature,[23] official website[24]
Monaco	Excluded from sample		
Montenegro	Judicial Council: Constitution of Montenegro (2007) gives the council powers over judicial careers (Art.128)	Yes (borderline case). 10 members, with 5 members elected by political actors, 4 members elected by peers, and the President being elected by the Council itself	Constitution, Cabufal project[25]

(continued)

---

[22] Bobek and Kosar (2014).
[23] Solomon (2018).
[24] https://www.csm.md/ro/despre-csm.html (accessed 10.09.2022).
[25] https://cabufal.ac.me/partners/judicial-council-of-montenegro-jc/ (accessed 10.09.2022).

Appendix A: Classification and Justification of Models of Judicial Governance 75

(continued)

Country	Model of Judicial Governance: justification	Independent organ for judicial governance (only possible when based on judicial council of courts service): justification (at least half of members must not be elected by political actors)	Sources
Netherlands	Courts Service: very limited competences on judicial careers	Yes: members are formally appointed by Minister of Justice, but at proposal of an independent body	Official website,[26] Judiciary Organization Act[27]
North Macedonia	Judicial Council: Law on Judicial Council gives the institution powers over judicial careers	Yes: Law on Judicial Council foresees that a majority (though not all) of members shall be elected by peers	Venice Commission,[28] official website[29]
Norway	Courts Service: see source	No: appointed by Parliament and by King-in-Council	Specialized literature,[30] official website
Poland	Judicial Council (weak): this is a borderline case. However, literature confirms that the institution has certain powers over judicial careers, which include powers to propose appointment and dismissal of 1st instance judges	No: most members politically appointed	Specialized literature[31,32]

(continued)

---

[26] https://www.rechtspraak.nl/English/The-Council-for-the-Judiciary#c9058a55-5cea-4ae7-ab46-8bf49767aa827268c952-b3a7-439c-9c95-c1a2dd66677a7 (accessedd 10.09.2022).

[27] https://www.rechtspraak.nl/SiteCollectionDocuments/Wet-op-de-Rechterlijke-Organisatie_EN.pdf (accessed 10.09.2022).

[28] https://www.venice.coe.int/webforms/documents/default.aspx?pdffile=CDL-REF(2018)028-E (accessed 10.09.2022).

[29] http://www.vsrm.mk/wps/portal/central/sud/sudski-sistem/sovet/!ut/p/z1/lZHNDoIwDICfxQN XWgUHeluiQBCDiU5xF4NmDhJgBFFeX4wn_Le3Nt_XNi1wiIAX8SWVcZ2qIs7afMvJjrimi fYMgxAdG-ncJ_MVmgY6Q9h0AXfBrBaYoLca-QPXIsD_8p-Bm49vguKjb3ukj3Q6Ga5D5hr UMX6b_2HAV59_W5F3e7xYsQs833ApCvCBy0zt7z-hxd6wJfBKHEUlKv1cteWkrsvTWE MNm6bRpVIyE_pB5Rq-UhJ1qiHqklDmjLEI00WSXQLa610BBS8NbQ!!/dz/d5/L0lHSkovd 0RNQUZrQUVnQSEhLzROVkUvbWs!/ (accessed 10.09.2022).

[30] Bobek and Kosar (2014).

[31] Castillo-Ortiz (2019).

[32] Sadurski (2019).

(continued)

Country	Model of Judicial Governance: justification	Independent organ for judicial governance (only possible when based on judicial council of courts service): justification (at least half of members must not be elected by political actors)	Sources
Portugal	Judicial Council: wide range of competences, including over judicial careers	No: a slight majority of members are politically appointed	ENCJ factsheets, official website[33] Specialized literature[34]
Romania	Judicial Council: wide competences over judicial careers	Yes: majority of judges and prosecutors elected by peers (albeit validated by Senate)	ENCJ factsheet, official website[35]
Russia	Hybrid/Other: there is a Council of the Judiciary, but political actors retain significant powers over judicial careers. Additionally, a Qualification Collegia also has powers over judicial careers	No: not based on judicial council or courts service models (a majority of members of the judicial council and of the Qualification Collegia is appointed by the All-Russia Council of Judges). However, political actors retain powers over judicial careers	Constitution UN Special Rapporteur on the independence of judges and lawyers[36]
San Marino	Excluded from sample		
Serbia	Judicial Council: Constitution gives the council powers over judicial careers	No: a majority of members appointed by political actors, although a draft reform to have half of members appointed by peer judges had been proposed	Constitution, official website[37]

(continued)

---

[33] https://www.csm.org.pt/vogais/ (10.09.2022).

[34] Castillo-Ortiz (2017).

[35] https://www.csm1909.ro/Default.aspx (10.09.2022).

[36] https://www2.ohchr.org/english/bodies/hrcouncil/docs/11session/A.HRC.11.41.Add.2_en.pdf (accessed 10.09.2022).

[37] https://www.vk.sud.rs/en/about-high-court-council (accessed 10.09.2022).

Appendix A: Classification and Justification of Models of Judicial Governance 77

(continued)

Country	Model of Judicial Governance: justification	Independent organ for judicial governance (only possible when based on judicial council of courts service): justification (at least half of members must not be elected by political actors)	Sources
Slovakia	Judicial Council: wide range of powers over careers of judges	Yes: half of members appointed by peer judges	Official website[38]
Slovenia	Judicial Council: wide range of powers over judicial careers	Yes: majority of members appointed by peer judges	Official website[39]
Spain	Judicial Council: wide range of powers over judicial careers	No: members appointed by the parliament	Official website[40]
Sweden	Courts Service: see source	No: directed by a Director General appointed by the Government	Specialized literature,[41] CCJE[42]
Switzerland	Hybrid/Other: see source	No: as this country follows a different, sui generis approach to judicial governance	Specialized literature[43]
Turkey	Judicial Council: Art.159 of the Constitution gives the institution powers over judicial careers	No: from 2017 most members elected by political actors	Constitution[44]

(continued)

---

[38] https://www.sudnarada.gov.sk/composition/?csrt=11364783616759360880 (accessed 10.09.2022).

[39] https://www.gov.si/en/state-authorities/other-institutions/judicial-council/ (accessed 10.09.2022).

[40] https://www.poderjudicial.es/cgpj/ (accessed 10.09.2022).

[41] Bobek and Kosar (2014).

[42] https://rm.coe.int/2017-report-situation-ofjudges-in-member-states/1680786ae1 (accessed 10.09.2022).

[43] Bobek and Kosar (2014).

[44] Çalı and Durmuş (2018), p. 1683.

(continued)

Country	Model of Judicial Governance: justification	Independent organ for judicial governance (only possible when based on judicial council of courts service): justification (at least half of members must not be elected by political actors)	Sources
UK (Includes the separate organs for judicial governance of England and Wales, Scotland and Northern Ireland)	Courts Service in all three cases: see source	Yes, although the cases have frequent traces of hybridity, in the Northern Irish Courts and Tribunals Service, the Lady Chief Justice appoints four judicial members of the board, and in addition, there are eight additional members. The Lady Chief Justice is appointed at the proposal of the Prime Minister but after consultation with the existing Lord Chief Justice and the Judicial Appointments Commission, which make a recommendation for appointment based on merit. In the Scottish Courts and Tribunal Service, most are either members ex officio or not politically appointed. In Her Majesty Courts and Tribunals Service (England and Wales), there are members ex officio and members approved by the Lord Chief Justice and the Lord Chancellor, although the Lord Chief Justice has a more protagonist role. Note, in addition, the existence of judges' councils in these jurisdictions	Specialized literature,[45,46] NICTS official website[47] SCTS official website[48] HMCTS Framework Document[49]

(continued)

[45] Castillo-Ortiz (2019).
[46] Castillo-Ortiz (2017).
[47] https://www.justice-ni.gov.uk/articles/nicts-agency-board-0 (10.09.2022).
[48] https://www.scotcourts.gov.uk/about-the-scottish-court-service/the-scottish-court-service-board (10.09.2022).
[49] https://assets.publishing.service.gov.uk/government/uploads/system/uploads/attachment_data/file/384922/hmcts-framework-document-2014.pdf (10.09.2022).

(continued)

Country	Model of Judicial Governance: justification	Independent organ for judicial governance (only possible when based on judicial council of courts service): justification (at least half of members must not be elected by political actors)	Sources
Ukraine	Judicial Council: powers over judicial careers	Yes: 21 members, of which 10 are appointed by peer judges plus 1 being the Chair of the Supreme Court serving ex officio	Specialized literature[50]
Vatican City	Excluded from sample		

JS2016: Justice Scoreboard 2016.

---

[50] Popova and Beers (2020).

Appendix B
Database for Replication of Statistical Analyses

Country	JudGover	JudiGoverInde	JudicialC	Cservice	Ministry	HybridOther	IndepJGov	IndepJudicialC	DepJudicialC	GDP
Albania	1	1	1	0	0	0	1	1	0	13,295.41
Armenia	4	6	0	0	0	1		0	0	12,592.64
Austria	3	5	0	0	1	0		0	0	51,935.6
Azerbaijan	4	6	0	0	0	1		0	0	13,699.67
Belarus	3	5	0	0	1	0		0	0	19,148.18
Belgium	2	3	0	1	0	0	1	0	0	48,210.03
Bosnia and Herzegovina	1	1	1	0	0	0	1	1	0	14,339.83
Bulgaria	1	1	1	0	0	0	1	1	0	22,383.81
Croatia	1	1	1	0	0	0	1	1	0	26,465.13
Cyprus	4	6	0	0	0	1		0	0	37,655.18
Czechia	3	5	0	0	1	0		0	0	38,319.34
Denmark	2	3	0	1	0	0	1	0	0	55,938.21
Estonia	1	1	1	0	0	0	1	1	0	35,638.42
Finland	2	4	0	1	0	0	0	0	0	47,260.8
France	1	1	1	0	0	0	1	1	0	42,025.62
Georgia	1	1	1	0	0	0	1	1	0	14,089.3
Germany	3	5	0	0	1	0		0	0	50,922.36
Greece	1	1	1	0	0	0	1	1	0	27,287.08
Hungary	4	6	0	0	0	1		0	0	31,007.77
Iceland	2	3	0	1	0	0	1	0	0	52,279.73

(continued)

Appendix B: Database for Replication of Statistical Analyses 83

(continued)

Country	JudGover	JudiGoverInde	JudicialC	Cservice	Ministry	HybridOther	IndepJGov	IndepJudicialC	DepJudicialC	GDP
Ireland	2	3	0	1	0	0	1	0	0	89,688.96
Italy	1	1	1	0	0	0	1	1	0	38,992.15
Kazakhstan	4	6	0	0	0	1		0	0	25,337.15
Kosovo	1	1	1	0	0	0	1	1	0	10,776.1
Latvia	2	3	0	1	0	0	1	0	0	29,932.49
Lithuania	1	1	1	0	0	0	1	1	0	36,732.03
Luxembourg	4	6	0	0	0	1		0	0	110,261.2
Malta	2	3	0	1	0	0	1	0	0	39,222.14
Moldova	1	1	1	0	0	0	1	1	0	12,324.74
Montenegro	1	1	1	0	0	0	1	1	0	18,278.73
Netherlands	2	3	0	1	0	0	1	0	0	54,209.56
NorthMacedonia	1	1	1	0	0	0	1	1	0	15,848.42
Norway	2	4	0	1	0	0	0	0	0	63,585.9
Poland	1	2	1	0	0	0	0	0	1	32,238.16
Portugal	1	2	1	0	0	0	0	0	1	32,181.15
Romania	1	1	1	0	0	0	1	1	0	28,832.62
Russia	4	6	0	0	0	1		0	0	26,456.39
Serbia	1	2	1	0	0	0	0	0	1	18,210
Slovakia	1	1	1	0	0	0	1	1	0	30,330.04
Slovenia	1	1	1	0	0	0	1	1	0	36,547.74

(continued)

(continued)

Country	JudGover	JudiGoverInde	JudicialC	Cservice	Ministry	HybridOther	IndepJGov	IndepJudicialC	Historic_LibDem	DepJudicialC	ReinstateConst	GDP
Spain	1	2	1	0	0	0	0	0		1	0	36,215.45
Sweden	2	4	0	1	0	0	0	0		0	0	50,683.32
Switzerland	4	6	0	0	0	1		0		0	1	68,393.31
Turkey	1	2	1	0	0	0	0	0		1	0	28,384.99
Ukraine	1	1	1	0	0	0	1	1		0	0	12,377.02
UnitedK	2	3	0	1	0	0	1	0		0	0	41,627.13

Country	judicorrupt	v2x_libdem	v2x_polyarchy	v2xcl_rol	v2juhcind	EU_MS	Current_LibDem					
Albania	0.33	0.403	0.501	0.901	0.351	0	0		0		0	
Armenia		0.597	0.786	0.885	0.632	0	1		0		0	
Austria	0.93	0.758	0.842	0.948	2.541	1	1		0		1	
Azerbaijan		0.066	0.201	0.365	−2.779	0	0		0		0	
Belarus	0.71	0.076	0.236	0.19	−2.837	0	0		0		0	
Belgium	0.94	0.821	0.887	0.977	1.761	1	1		0		1	
Bosnia and Herzegovina	0.53	0.34	0.545	0.753	1.031	0	0		0		0	
Bulgaria	0.58	0.491	0.603	0.873	0.709	1	0		0		0	
Croatia	0.71	0.641	0.753	0.859	0.751	1	1		0		0	
Cyprus	0.9	0.724	0.825	0.943	1.184	1	1		0		0	
Czechia	0.87	0.708	0.805	0.939	1.774	1	1		0		0	
Denmark	0.99	0.878	0.91	0.975	2.841	1	1		0		0	
Estonia	0.95	0.832	0.89	0.976	1.609	1	1		0		0	

(continued)

Appendix B: Database for Replication of Statistical Analyses

(continued)

Country	judicorrupt	v2x_libdem	v2x_polyarchy	v2xcl_rol	v2juhcind	EU_MS	Current_LibDem	Historic_LibDem	ReinstateConst
Finland	0.98	0.837	0.878	0.983	2.277	1	1	0	0
France	0.9	0.796	0.877	0.948	1.611	1	1	0	0
Georgia	0.72	0.506	0.643	0.89	0.754	0	1	0	0
Germany	0.95	0.833	0.879	0.988	1.884	1	1	0	0
Greece	0.81	0.744	0.843	0.951	1.393	1	1	0	0
Hungary	0.67	0.368	0.467	0.893	0.218	1	0	0	0
Iceland		0.79	0.854	0.965	2.441	0	1	1	
Ireland	0.98	0.817	0.881	0.98	2.485	1	1	1	0
Italy	0.81	0.785	0.861	0.94	1.386	1	1	0	0
Kazakhstan	0.58	0.129	0.24	0.61	−1.699	0	0	0	0
Kosovo	0.46	0.43	0.611	0.727	0.901	0	0	0	1
Latvia	0.81	0.736	0.821	0.957	3.364	1	1	0	0
Lithuania	0.83	0.76	0.821	0.943	2.687	1	1	0	0
Luxembourg	0.95	0.783	0.869	0.946	1.718	1	1	0	0
Malta	0.88	0.612	0.772	0.923	1.624	1	1	0	0
Moldova	0.41	0.467	0.623	0.776	1.339	0	0	0	0
Montenegro		0.347	0.454	0.729	0.331	0	0	0	0
Netherlands	0.97	0.825	0.87	0.965	1.863	1	1	0	1
NorthMacedonia	0.51	0.428	0.633	0.803	−0.429	0	0	0	0
Norway	0.98	0.855	0.899	0.958	2.701	0	1	0	1

(continued)

(continued)

Country	judicorrupt	v2x_libdem	v2x_polyarchy	v2xcl_rol	v2juhcind	EU_MS	Current_LibDem	Historic_LibDem	ReinstateConst
Poland	0.87	0.487	0.632	0.836	0.425	1	0	0	0
Portugal	0.87	0.792	0.876	0.907	1.961	1	1	0	0
Romania	0.71	0.552	0.76	0.821	1.987	1	1	0	0
Russia	0.54	0.104	0.261	0.49	−2.581	0	0	0	0
Serbia	0.5	0.239	0.342	0.803	0.075	0	0	0	0
Slovakia	0.57	0.756	0.836	0.913	2.237	1	1	0	0
Slovenia	0.78	0.651	0.748	0.906	2.019	1	1	0	0
Spain	0.88	0.8	0.886	0.983	2.096	1	1	0	0
Sweden	0.97	0.873	0.905	0.984	2.803	1	1	1	
Switzerland		0.847	0.892	0.98	2.908	0	1	1	
Turkey	0.57	0.111	0.286	0.243	0.075	0	0	0	0
Ukraine	0.48	0.348	0.544	0.718	0.015	0	0	0	0
UnitedK	0.96	0.797	0.872	0.922	2.147	0	1	1	

Appendix C
QCA Data Matrix for Replication of Analyses

Appendix C: QCA Data Matrix for Replication of Analyses

Country	IndepJudicialC	GDP	Judicorrupt	v2x_polyarchy	Polyx100	Outchigh	Outcmed	Outclow	v2juhcind	EU_MS	HighcourtF	gdpF	NocorrupCAL
Albania	1	13,295.4	0.33	0.501	501	0	1	0	0.351	0	0.61	0.08	0.07
Armenia	0	12,592.6		0.786	786	1	0	0	0.632	0	0.67	0.07	
Austria	0	51,935.6	0.93	0.842	842	1	0	0	2.541	1	0.93	0.96	0.99
Azerbaijan	0	13,699.7		0.201	201	0	0	1	−2.779	0	0.06	0.08	
Belarus	0	19,148.2	0.71	0.236	236	0	0	1	−2.837	0	0.06	0.16	0.89
Belgium	0	48,210	0.94	0.887	887	1	0	0	1.761	1	0.86	0.94	0.99
BiH	1	14,339.8	0.53	0.545	545	0	1	0	1.031	0	0.75	0.09	0.55
Bulgaria	1	22,383.8	0.58	0.603	603	0	1	0	0.709	1	0.69	0.24	0.67
Croatia	1	26,465.1	0.71	0.753	753	1	0	0	0.751	1	0.69	0.37	0.89
Cyprus	0	37,655.2	0.9	0.825	825	1	0	0	1.184	1	0.78	0.76	0.98
Czechia	0	38,319.3	0.87	0.805	805	1	0	0	1.774	1	0.86	0.78	0.98
Denmark	0	55,938.2	0.99	0.91	910	1	0	0	2.841	1	0.95	0.98	0.99
Estonia	1	35,638.4	0.95	0.89	890	1	0	0	1.609	1	0.84	0.7	0.99
Finland	0	47,260.8	0.98	0.878	878	1	0	0	2.277	1	0.91	0.93	0.99
France	1	42,025.6	0.9	0.877	877	1	0	0	1.611	1	0.84	0.86	0.98
Georgia	1	14,089.3	0.72	0.643	643	0	1	0	0.754	0	0.7	0.08	0.9
Germany	0	50,922.4	0.95	0.879	879	1	0	0	1.884	1	0.87	0.96	0.99
Greece	1	27,287.1	0.81	0.843	843	1	0	0	1.393	1	0.81	0.4	0.96
Hungary	0	31,007.8	0.67	0.467	467	0	1	0	0.218	1	0.58	0.54	0.84
Iceland	0	52,279.7		0.854	854	1	0	0	2.441	0	0.92	0.97	
Ireland	0	89,689	0.98	0.881	881	1	0	0	2.485	1	0.92	1	0.99
Italy	1	38,992.1	0.81	0.861	861	1	0	0	1.386	1	0.81	0.79	0.96
Kazakhstan	0	25,337.2	0.58	0.24	240	0	0	1	−1.699	0	0.16	0.33	0.67
Kosovo	1	10,776.1	0.46	0.611	611	0	1	0	0.901	0	0.72	0.05	0.33

(continued)

Appendix C: QCA Data Matrix for Replication of Analyses

(continued)

Latvia	0	29,932.5	0.81	0.821	821	1	0	0	3.364	1	0.97	0.5	0.96
Lithuania	1	36,732	0.83	0.821	821	1	0	0	2.687	1	0.94	0.73	0.96
Luxembourg	0	110,261	0.95	0.869	869	1	0	0	1.718	1	0.85	1	0.99
Malta	0	39,222.1	0.88	0.772	772	1	0	0	1.624	1	0.84	0.8	0.98
Moldova	1	12,324.7	0.41	0.623	623	0	1	0	1.339	0	0.8	0.07	0.19
Montenegro	1	18,278.7		0.454	454	0	1	0	0.331	0	0.6	0.15	
Netherlands	0	54,209.6	0.97	0.87	870	1	0	0	1.863	1	0.87	0.97	0.99
NorthMacedonia	1	15,848.4	0.51	0.633	633	0	1	0	−0.429	0	0.42	0.11	0.5
Norway	0	63,585.9	0.98	0.899	899	1	0	0	2.701	0	0.94	0.99	0.99
Poland	0	32,238.2	0.87	0.632	632	0	1	0	0.425	1	0.62	0.58	0.98
Portugal	0	32,181.2	0.87	0.876	876	1	0	0	1.961	1	0.88	0.58	0.98
Romania	1	28,832.6	0.71	0.76	760	1	0	0	1.987	1	0.88	0.46	0.89
Russia	0	26,456.4	0.54	0.261	261	0	0	1	−2.581	0	0.07	0.37	0.58
Serbia	0	18,210	0.5	0.342	342	0	0	1	0.075	0	0.54	0.15	0.46
Slovakia	1	30,330	0.57	0.836	836	1	0	0	2.237	1	0.91	0.51	0.65
Slovenia	1	36,547.7	0.78	0.748	748	1	0	0	2.019	1	0.89	0.73	0.94
Spain	0	36,215.4	0.88	0.886	886	1	0	0	2.096	1	0.89	0.72	0.98
Sweden	0	50,683.3	0.97	0.905	905	1	0	0	2.803	1	0.94	0.96	0.99
Switzerland	0	68,393.3		0.892	892	1	0	0	2.908	0	0.95	1	
Turkey	0	28,385	0.57	0.286	286	0	0	1	0.075	0	0.54	0.44	0.65
Ukraine	1	12,377	0.48	0.544	544	0	1	0	0.015	0	0.53	0.07	0.39
UnitedK	0	41,627.1	0.96	0.872	872	1	0	0	2.147	0	0.9	0.85	0.99

References

Bobek M, Kosar D (2014) Global solutions, local damages: a critical study in judicial councils in central and Eastern Europe. Ger Law J 15:1257–1292

Çalı B, Durmuş B (2018) Judicial self-government as experimental constitutional politics: the case of Turkey. Ger Law J 19:1671–1706. https://doi.org/10.1017/S2071832200023208

Castillo-Ortiz PJ (2017) Councils of the judiciary and judges' perceptions of respect to their independence in Europe. Hague J Rule Law 9:315–336. https://doi.org/10.1007/s40803-017-0061-2

Castillo-Ortiz P (2019) The politics of implementation of the judicial council model in Europe. Eur Polit Sci Rev 11:503–520. https://doi.org/10.1017/S1755773919000298

European Commission, Directorate-General for Justice and Consumers (2016) The 2016 EU justice scoreboard. Publications Office, Luxembourg

OECD (2019) OECD investment policy reviews: Croatia 2019

Popova M, Beers DJ (2020) No revolution of dignity for Ukraine's judges: judicial reform after the Euromaidan. demokratizatsiya 28:113–142

Sadurski W (2019) Poland's constitutional breakdown. Oxford University Press

Solomon PH (2018) Transparency in the work of judicial councils: the experience of (east) European countries. Rev Cent East Eur Law 43:43–62. https://doi.org/10.1163/15730352-04301003

Szente Z (2021) Stepping into the same river twice? Judicial independence in old and new authoritarianism. Ger Law J 22:1316–1326. https://doi.org/10.1017/glj.2021.69

The manufacturer's authorised representative in the EU is Springer Nature Customer Service Centre GmbH, Europaplatz 3, 69115 Heidelberg, Germany. If you have any concerns regarding our products, please contact ProductSafety@springernature.com

Printed and bound by CPI Group (UK) Ltd, Croydon, CR0 4YY

25/03/2026

02078172-0016